LANDMINES IN CAMBODIA

Landmines in Cambodia

Past, Present, and Future

Wade C. Roberts

CAMBRIA PRESS

Amherst, New York

Requests for permission should be directed to:
permissions@cambriapress.com, or mailed to:
Cambria Press
20 Northpointe Parkway, Suite 188
Amherst, NY 14228

Library of Congress Cataloging-in-Publication Data

Roberts, Wade C.
Landmines in Cambodia : past, present, and future /
Wade C. Roberts.
p. cm.
Includes bibliographical references and index.
ISBN 978-1-60497-761-5 (alk. paper)
1. Land mines—Cambodia. 2. Land mines— Detection—Cambodia.
3. Land mine victims— Cambodia. 4. Unexploded ordnance—
Economic aspects—Cambodia. 5. Cambodia—Economic
conditions. 6. Cambodia—History--1975-1979.
7. Cambodia—History—1979- I. Title.

UG490.R64 2011
363.34—dc22

2011007770

To my loving parents Mike and Janine;
my children Bronson, Tyus, and Ajia;
and, most critically, my research partner
and eternal companion, Cindy

Landmines Beneath Me
by U Sam Oeur

I wade through solitude
To the cottage where we used to
Gather to drink rice wine,
Enjoying false peace.

I sit under the same palm-leaf roof,
Gaze at your chairs
But see no one,
Hear only your laughs.

Here, it's like everywhere else—
Deserted,
Villages of black roofless houses;
I don't see even one dog.

The explosions of mines,
The roaring of heavy artillery
From frontier to frontier, shake every
Grain of pollen from the Champa flowers.

I cannot move for fear of death
I must move forward to avoid death
Death,
Seems certain, landmines beneath my feet.

No place to hide, no skies under which to rest;
And the moaning of children,
And the cries of mothers
Out of blazing fire across the land,

And your bodies, brothers, shielding us
From the bullets, and your blood
Splashing over our Mother, induce my soul
To ever worship Jasmine and Lotus blossoms.

The Price of Water in Cambodia.

Source. Photo Taken by author in Pailin Province Cambodia, March 2008.

Table of Contents

List of Figures

List of Tables

Preface

My motodriver (driver of a taxi service using a small motorcycle) leaned over his right shoulder, announcing that the road was about to turn very bumpy. I squinted with one eye in order to gain sight of Cambodia's landscape through the dusty lens of my video camera. The residual smells of harvested rice lingered in the air. Palm trees stood as barriers, dividing one farmer's field from the next. Small one-room huts providing shelter for a dozen people were positioned in close proximity to the slender street. Behind homes were the fields where the able-bodied labored during sunlight hours. Barefoot children coaxed cows toward a predetermined target. Women wearing colorful sarongs balanced baskets of treasures on their heads as they made their way to local markets. The aged sat beneath the stilt-supported huts, basking in the shadows provided by the wooden slats.

Cambodia is a land of contrast: astonishing temples and deficient aqueducts, elegant dance and pervasive disease, grandeur and genocide, prosperity and poverty, landmarks and landmines. Every village has a story, every family a trial. Life is fragile and death is commonplace.

Religious and cultural institutions give cognitive pacification when crop failures occur or new mothers die during childbirth. The traditions here are strong and people have discovered ways to endure. While most survive, the majority does so in chronic and pervasive poverty. Economic need is profuse. My eyes are continually opened to the consequences of destitution. My heart hurts. How was I so lucky? If the situation were reversed, would anyone be willing to come to my aid? It would be so easy to turn away. Perhaps, with time, I would forget these feelings of responsibility.

By midmorning, we had ventured beyond the village where we had spent the past several days. Each passing ridge provided a more picturesque view than the last. We stopped to talk to travelers making their journeys on foot. Each person seemed helpful in giving us the needed information to continue our voyage. I found myself looking for crop selection patterns as we slowly traversed past fields of cassava, soybean, and sweet potato. No astonishing blueprint was discovered. Observing the passing fields in this way drew attention to fields that were unplanted or overgrown with weeds. If people were going hungry, why not plant seeds in every field? Closer scrutiny satisfied my query. Unplanted fields were marked with placards reading "DANGER MINES!" These words, written in both English and the local language, were positioned on a metal rectangle, illuminated with a brilliant red backdrop, and hoisted on a bamboo pole to a height that would likely alert a passerby to the present danger. A skull with crossing bones was pictured in the center of the design. The untamed expansion of the landmine-laden fields occasionally concealed the visibility of the warning placards from the roadsides view. With a little bit of practice, I was able to discover the next red sign, having noted typical placement practices. DANGER MINES! DANGER MINES! DANGER MINES! The signs were everywhere.

A young boy walking near one of these signs caught my eye. I asked my motodriver to pull to the side of the road. My hands went into an automatic mode of attaching a long-range lens to my camera while my legs scurried toward a position that would facilitate the perfect picture. I sat quietly. I wondered why anyone would risk walking through such dangerous terrain. He was carrying two containers. The first was a rather small container positioned beneath his left arm, balancing on his hip. This container, with a bright yellow label wrapped around its body, was likely used for some liquid substance at one time. The second container, much larger in size, was likely an old water canister. A swell of mud shifted back and forth in the bottom of the container as he swung the gallon-size jug with the cadence of his gait. He sensed someone was watching him. He turned in my direction. I snapped the image. The boy continued a short way, filled his canisters with water, and made his journey back in the direction of his approach.

The combination of extreme rains and flat dirt roads was a perfect recipe for potholes. As we swerved in and out in an effort to avoid the dents and dips the road presented as obstacles, I compared travel in my home country to my current experience. Was everything more difficult here? I marveled at how Cambodia was burdened with explosive remnants of war decades beyond war. Traversing the unmarked paths eventually led us to our desired location—a village near the Cambodia–Vietnam border. Now we needed to find someone searching for metal. It did not take long.

Sarun Sot was standing in an open field outfitted with a worn sack dangling from one shoulder. On his other shoulder, he had positioned a strap which was connected to the shaft of a metal detector. The strap helped to hold the weight of the device as he motioned it left and right in concentrically expanding semicircle patterns. Alone, he was searching for metal. Sarun was 12 years old. His family relied on the income he acquired selling the snippets and oddments of metal he unearthed. He would tote his daily find to his uncle's home less than a kilometer away from where he lived. After being paid the going rate for the weight of metal he had uncovered, he quickly instituted the return leg of his journey toward his home with cash in hand. A portion of his earnings was given to pay rent on the metal detector. The remainder was handed over to his father. Sarun was to continue this process the following day, and the next, and the next. No long-term escape plan was in place.

We had now journeyed through dozens of villages. Our journey started in the northwest province of Banteay Mean Chey and meandered toward the southeast province of Svay Rieng. In each village, we were able to chronicle a similar account. Situations of poverty and economic need often induced risky behavior involving explosive remnants of war. Most often, this interaction was intentional in an effort to temporarily ameliorate the sting of poverty. It was Sarun's plight that motivated my research. Sarun died July 14, 2008. He was not alone in his fate. His providence was shared with more than 63,000 others.

The vast majority of landmine-related incidents (i.e., accidents and tampering) occurring in Cambodia today are consequences of intentional tampering. How is tampering influenced by poverty and economic need? Do correlations exist between agricultural vulnerability and tampering behavior? Are people responding to metal price incentives and seeking ordnance when the price of metal is high? Answers to these questions are provided in this book. Numerous significant correlations discovered in this book will facilitate a more targeted approach to combating the residual ordnance problem in Cambodia.

Sarun asked me about where I was from. I found it difficult to elaborate on the details of my upbringing. I described snow and the expansive interstate highways. I permitted my hands to assist me in explaining a rollercoaster one would encounter when visiting a theme park. I detailed my experience with competitive swimming in college. His intrigue was coupled with an understanding that he would never be a part of my world. I had acquired the factual information necessary to perform the desired statistical analyses. Moreover, I was extremely privileged to meet and become friends with several wonderful people. This meant it was time to return home. As I reflected on my notes from each of the research trips taken, my heart was left heavy. As geography quickly became a gaping chasm separating me physically from Cambodia, I reflected on the vast distinctions between the two worlds. I was returning to a world of privilege and prospect, literally walking away from pervasive poverty and its consequences. It was no longer easy to walk away.

Acknowledgments

Throughout the research and writing of this book, I have benefited greatly from the combined efforts of academic scholars, generosity of financial contributors, support of family and friends, contributions of Cambodian individuals and organizations, and the leading hand of God.

Prior to graduate school, I spent 2 years living with Cambodian refugees who fled from the ominous Khmer Rouge regime. I gained a love for the Cambodian people and a passion for the developing world. I owe a debt of gratitude to Kirk Powell, Coach Mike Werner, and Coach Dennis Tesch, who led me to believe in myself and gave me the courage that allowed me to undertake such an endeavor. I also wish to express appreciation to Dr. Günseli Berik, who taught an influential course in development economics and directed me toward graduate school. I wish to thank her for setting my academic pursuits on a beautiful and meaningful course.

In regard to the research for this book, I would like to extend special thanks to Dr. Cihan Bilginsoy, who provided priceless insights into this work and has become a lifelong friend. I would also like to thank the University of

Utah economics department for the requisite training in various fields of economics that helped to facilitate this work. I also would like to thank Dr. Richard Fowles, Dr. Thomas Maloney, Dr. Zackary Zimmer, and Dr. Norman Waitzman, who have all contributed to this work in unique ways. Additionally, I would like to extend appreciation to the reviewer of this book, who provided numerous insights and improvement suggestions.

This research has also benefited from the financial assistance of the University of Utah economics department, the Marriner S. Eccles Foundation, Solvay Pharmaceuticals, and thousands of private swim lessons. Most critically, this work became financially possible because of the sacrifices of my wife and both my parents. My wife, Cindy, who willingly assisted in selling our home to finance research trips, and my parents, who allowed us to live in their home, provided the conduit by which the research for this book became possible.

I express a deep-felt gratitude for the structure of family support that has enabled and supported my various goals and aspirations. Cindy not only supported me throughout this process but also became an active participant in the cause, accompanying me on research trips, learning the Cambodian tongue, and contributing greatly to the work. Her efforts, ambition, and love for the Cambodian people will lead to exciting projects in the future.

Countless interviews with and contributions from CMVIS, CMAC, CMAA, RGC, various other ministries, and individuals have also helped to develop this work. I wish to thank the people of Cambodia for their acceptance and willingness to assist in this cause. Thank you for your kind hearts and open homes. I stand awestruck at the trials you have endured and the humility with which you continue forward.

Finally, I wish to recognize the hand of God that guided this work through every stage. Though I have never personally experienced starvation, severe poverty, destitution, a landmine explosion, or death, I now know of their existence firsthand. I believe we all have a responsibility to become part of the solution. As Eleanor Powell so appropriately puts it, "What we are is God's gift to us. What we become is our gift to God."

Landmines in Cambodia

Chapter 1

History and Consequence

> If you desire to understand today, you have to start by searching yesterday.
>
> —Pearl Buck

1.1. Introduction

Throughout the past century, Cambodians have endured colonial occupations by the French and the Vietnamese, US bombing raids, genocide by the Khmer Rouge, and civil war lasting more than 20 years. Cambodians have also had to deal with agricultural droughts and floods, starvation, disease, human trafficking, resource exploitation by foreign powers, involuntary repatriation movements, and the ever-present danger of encountering landmines and unexploded ordnance (UXO).

Cambodia is a poor, agrarian-based country. GDP per capita in Cambodia was US$385 in 2005 (National Institute of Statistics [NIS] 2006). Agricultural output accounted for 29% of the GDP in 2007 but involved 60% of the labor force. Life expectancy at birth in 2007 stood at 61.3 years. The vast majority of deaths under the age of 5 (68%) occur as a result of neonatal conditions, diarrhea, and pneumonia. Individuals surviving the first 5 years of life are most likely to encounter death as a consequence of HIV (10%), tuberculosis (8%), and diarrhea (7%). In comparison to these problems, landmine- and UXO-related incidents pose less significant threats to human lives. For those encountering landmine-related ordnance, however, the ramifications are endless.

It is likely that the country of Cambodia is the only country in the world to have more active landmines buried beneath the ground than people living above it.[1] In addition to the landmine problem, residual UXO litters the country with an estimated 324,000 tons of postwar explosives. While estimations about the number of active landmines and residual UXO remaining in the country vary, even the most conservative estimates place Cambodia at a decisive disadvantage when considering ordnance estimations in relation to the population of the country.

In total, 58,000 individuals have suffered maiming, amputation, and/or death in relation to landmines/UXO since 1980. Between 1980 and 1998, an annual average of 2,700 landmine/UXO incidents took place, a number that declined to 781 between 1999 and 2007. The presence of ordnance prevents land from being used in harvest cycles and encourages the utilization of less-productive land in agricultural efforts. Individuals surviving an encounter with landmines/UXO often struggle to survive among a myriad of problems ranging from psychological to physical. When individuals suffer an ordnance incident, family members typically already experiencing extreme poverty are often forced into assuming debt, prostituting their daughters, and separating from each other to seek the aid of an international donor.

Despite the decrease in absolute ordnance numbers, landmine-related incidents still occur daily in Cambodia, leaving individuals maimed, with amputated limbs, or dead. People continue to walk past warning plaques to forage for food and gather water. On their way to school, children often cross fields suspected of being contaminated. Individuals migrating to new areas forcibly accept landmine risks with the allocation of land. The poor even intentionally seek ordnance, ironically to "afford" another day of life. When individuals experience an ordnance-related incident, their lives—and the lives of their families—are forever impacted.

Critical distinctions exist between landmines and UXO. Landmines are designed to maim and are strategically positioned beneath the earth's surface in locations critical during war efforts. Ordnance parcels, on the other hand, are designed to kill and wreak havoc. Residual UXO in Cambodia (also referred to as ordnance parcels in this report) primarily entails unexploded ordnance parcels dropped from airplanes during the Vietnam era. Landmines and UXO are not only distinct in their design but also in their locations within Cambodia. The distinction between these two types of ordnance is complicated due to a language oversight in the Cambodian tongue. *Krop mean*, referring to a mine, is a term often used collectively for all types of ordnance. As Cambodians gain more experience with ordnance, however, language is slowly adapting to distinguish between landmines and residual ordnance contamination. Specifically, the term *krop mean* includes a classifying term, *min pteu*, meaning "without explosion," to refer to UXO. This distinction, however, is not universally made.

Landmines and UXO in Cambodia are distinct from one another with regard to where they are, how they injure people, and in how they are discovered. In light of these factors, this book examines landmines and UXO in both separate and aggregated measures in an effort to test for statistical distinctions for specific ordnance types.

The objective of this book is to examine the relationship between the frequency of civilian landmine/UXO incidents and socioeconomic, agriculturally specific, and economic conditions over the 1980 to 2007 period in Cambodia. I estimate statistically how poverty, demographic conditions, agricultural fluctuations, and the price of scrap metal affect the prevalence of both landmine and UXO incident rates. Landmine/UXO incidents are disaggregated into accidents and tampering incidents throughout each analysis. Findings of this exercise are expected to inform current attempts of the landmine/UXO governmental and nongovernmental organizations currently working on ameliorating the impact of ordnance.

The remainder of this chapter is organized as follows: Section 1.2 explains the methodology that will be used in the book. Section 1.3

discusses data sources used. Section 1.4 outlines the plan of the book. Section 1.5 details the existing literature on ordnance in Cambodia. Section 1.6 provides historical information leading up to the current ordnance problem. Section 1.7 summarizes the impact ordnance has had on specific groups of people. Section 1.8 details domestic and international actions that have been taken to combat the problem.

1.2. METHODOLOGY

This book uses cross-section, panel, and time-series estimation methods in testing hypotheses. Various measures of socioeconomic conditions are used in an effort to test the hypothesis that economic need and poverty directly affect landmine/UXO incidents. This analysis is carried out for the cross section of 185 administrative districts.

Next, an examination of the impact agricultural conditions have on landmine/UXO incidents takes place. This analysis takes place at a provincial level for every harvest season between 1998 and 2006. Administrative boundaries in Cambodia structure provinces as the first and largest unit of geographic division. Cambodia is currently composed of 26 provinces. It is my hypothesis that landmine/UXO incidents are directly related to levels of agricultural output.

Finally, a monthly time-series analysis is introduced, examining the relationship between the price of scrap metal and the prevalence of landmine/UXO incidents. This analysis takes place for the entire country between March 1996 and December 2007. Testing this hypothesis is possible for the first time following the acquisition of a price record near the Cambodia–Thailand border accomplished during the field research phase of this book. Accordingly, a paramount hypothesis relating tampering activities to the price of scrap metal is posed and statistically explored.

One important contribution of this book is the unique distinction made between accidents and tampering. While the distinction between these two incident types is traditionally made by ordnance type (landmines vs. UXO), I redefine tampering and, instead, consider economic incentives as the distinguishing characteristic that defines tampering. More specifically, tampering involves the intentional handling of ordnance whereas accidental incidents do not. I will demonstrate that the driving forces of the two types of incidents are different. For instance, tampering activities are expected to rise with the price of scrap metal, although this is not likely to be the case for accidents. The distinction is critical from a policy perspective because efforts taken to ameliorate incidents require the identification of conditions that increase the likelihood of each type of occurrence. The recently observed reversal in the relative share of accidents and tampering also underscores the importance of this separation.

1.3. Data Sources

Information regarding landmine/UXO incidents used throughout this book comes from the Cambodian Mine/UXO Victim Information System (CMVIS) database (CMVIS, 2008). CMVIS statistics are housed in Phnom Penh, Cambodia. This study utilizes the complete micro level dataset of individual-specific information. Summary statistics are available from CMVIS upon request. This data set is made up of individual-specific information for victims including names, incident dates, sex, age, incident location, incident activity, incident severity, and military status. This information, in various forms, serves as the dependent variable throughout this work. The CMVIS database is the culmination of incident information from various organizations throughout Cambodia.[2]

Information for poverty and various socioeconomic variables was collected from the 1998 General Census of Cambodia (NIS, 1998; Regional Government Cambodia 1999), the 1998 Population Census of Cambodia (NIS, 2004b), and the 2004 Cambodian Socioeconomic Survey (NIS, 2004a). Information regarding various measures of agricultural conditions was obtained from the Ministry of Agriculture in Phnom Penh. Data regarding the price of metal were obtained personally by conducting field research in Cambodia (2006–2009). This exclusive record is, in and of itself, a unique contribution to the landmine sector, enabling quantitative analysis regarding the price of metal and landmine/UXO tampering behavior in Cambodia. The price record can be obtained by contacting the author.

1.4. Book Outline

I first separate incident activities into three categories: agrarian-, traveling-, and tampering-related events. These categorical distinctions, which are expanded on in Chapter 2, are critical when discovering vulnerabilities that occur within each incident type. Following the division of incidents, historical background, and explanation within each incident category, the remainder of the book concentrates on the relationship between landmine/UXO incidents (disaggregated into accidents and tampering) socioeconomics, agricultural conditions, and the price of metal.

Chapter 3 presents a cross-section model testing accident and tampering rates against several measures of poverty and socioeconomic indicators. Socioeconomic measures include age dependence, single-parent dependence, formal education proportions, firewood–cooking proportions, safe drinking water proportions, K5 districts, migration, population densities, rural/urban status, and sex ratios. I hypothesize that landmine/UXO accidents and tampering incidents are linked to each of these variables in specific ways. Identifying these linkages will assist policy makers in formulating practical plans to preempt the occurrence of landmine/UXO incidents in the form of both accidents and tampering.

Chapter 4 tests various indicators of agricultural vulnerability against landmine/UXO accidents and tampering incidents in an effort to test the hypothesis that the number of incidents rises with increased rates of economic need arising from agricultural shortages. Measures of agricultural vulnerability included in this analysis comprise net rice values, supplies of water, the yield of specific rice varieties, crop diversification, the proportion of crop lost to natural disasters in the form of droughts, floods, and insect infestation, and the ability to substitute rice with other food products. Following formal testing, I propose several policies that will assist in reducing agricultural vulnerability, thus contributing to the reduction in landmine/UXO incidents.

Chapter 5 evaluates the landmine-related incident rate across time as a function of the price of metal. I test the hypothesis that as the price of metal increases, tampering activity also increases. In addition to observing the price of metal, I also control for seasonal effects, the impact of specific zones, and year effects. Formal policy suggestions follow the formal testing that takes place in this chapter.

1.5. Literature Review

The existing literature on landmines in Cambodia from an economic standpoint is quite limited. The work of three researchers stands out. First, Harris (2000) carried out a cost-benefit analysis in regard to landmine clearance in Cambodia. He concluded that the benefits of removing landmines in Cambodia were worth 2% of the costs. Next, Bottomley (2001) recommended training in the informal sector in an effort to reduce the risk of demining. Importantly, she delineated landmine/UXO incidents into categories that suggested a portion of incidents occurred as a result of economically driven incentive structures. Finally, Keeley (2006) paired the tools of economics with Mine Action (the efforts to combat problems related to landmines and residual ordnance worldwide, which was formalized by the 1997 Ottawa Treaty). His work was critical in shaping programs and applying principles of efficiency within the Mine Action sector. The contributions of these authors will now be considered in turn.

1.5.1. Harris (2000)

When the 14 governments and European Commission (EC) make decisions about funding efforts toward landmine/UXO rehabilitation, consideration is given to return-on-investment yields.[3] These decisions directly affect 84 countries and eight territories impacted by landmines and UXO.[4] Decisions regarding the selection of countries and organizations to fund are often complex and not transparent. While many components of this process may never be completely understood, the determination of return-on-investment yields follows the age-old approach entitled "foregone earnings." Whether speaking of prevention mechanisms that forestall landmine/UXO incidents from occurring or rehabilitation services allowing the maimed to rejoin the workforce, the benefit of one life saved has been valued in accordance with the amount an individual can earn throughout the remainder of his or her life. The most pervasive Cambodian report indicating the value of cleared land, saved medical expenses, and the increase in "human value" from lives saved originates from a report authored by Geoff Harris (2000).

Harris was initially concerned with whether landmine clearance was economically efficient in Cambodia. Harris made specific identification parameters regarding the benefits of landmine clearance. These parameters included the money not spent in the medical treatment of victims, increased agricultural production, and the quantified value of human lives saved from landmine-related incidents. The costs of demining were explicit and involved the exact dollar amount necessary to clear mines within Cambodia. The combined benefits were weighed against the costs of demining. The conclusion of Harris's analysis found the benefits of removing landmines in Cambodia were worth only 2% of the costs.

Following the practice of valuing lives according to an earning potential, Cambodians were valued at US$134 a year (Harris 2000). This finite figure was not substantial enough to outweigh the direct costs involved in the demining process. In addition to the low value of life established, Harris also concluded maimed individuals, having completed programs of rehabilitation, had a productive capacity half that of a "normal" person. Accordingly, a completely rehabilitated maimed individual was valued at a mere $67 a year. International organizations rarely perform the cost-benefit analysis themselves but instead base their decisions on summary statistics of studies conducted by others. Harris's influential cost-benefit analysis undervalues life and puts poor countries at a decisive disadvantage concerning funding.

The Harris report says removing landmines in Cambodia is not beneficial according to a cost-benefit analysis. In addition to the problems that exist in regard to the foregone earnings approach of valuing life, Harris also ignores that considerable variance exists regarding the value of land throughout Cambodia. Assuming a standard value of land ignores the fact that some areas are more productive than others. Therefore, it is likely that even according to Harris's methodology, some areas of Cambodia would be considered worthwhile to demine. The strength of marginal analysis is at the micro level, a reality completely ignored in the Harris report. This report discounts standard economic analysis, using a methodology that more closely reflects an accounting framework. Accounting, while useful in specific applications, is not well suited for capturing social or opportunity costs. The Harris report has had damning effects for Cambodia, effects that could have been avoided by using an economic framework.

1.5.2. Bottomley

In spite of pressure not to engage in informal demining activities, many farmers with contaminated land opt to demine the land and not wait years for the formal demining sector to address their needs. Bottomley (2003) addressed this issue and proposed a radical solution to the problem at hand. More specifically, she broached the controversial subject of informal mine clearance by villagers and argued that the most effective way of addressing village demining is not by simply transferring expertise or prohibiting such activity but by focusing on the underlying vulnerabilities that force people to take the risks. Attention is given to the fact that informal demining takes place, and regardless of the conclusions cost-benefit and marginal analyses reach, the actions of individuals suggest it is optimal and necessary to clear landmine-related contamination. The inability of mine-risk education (MRE) to prevent landmine/UXO incidents from occurring suggests villagers somehow find it optimal to continue passing warning signs and handling ordnance. Given this reality, Bottomley suggested altering MRE to include provision for training villagers how to demine and tamper with ordnance in a safer manner. This approach is not supported by formal funding dollars and is seen by many as immoral.

In spite of moral opposition on the part of many international donors, one organization in Cambodia, known as Company A (an alias to protect its identity), has implemented one of Bottomley's suggestions.[5] Specifically, Company A offers financial incentives when people discover landmine-related ordnance. Villagers are informed that when they find landmines/UXO, Company A will quickly acquire the ordnance and compensate the villager according to the weight of the parcel. While this practice ultimately increases the rate at which people search for landmines/UXO, rates of incident occurrence have actually been dramatically reduced since its implementation.

Bottomley's work makes an important contribution to Mine Action in Cambodia in that it broadly distinguishes between two types of landmine/UXO incidents: those that occur as a result of intentional engagement and those that do not. This connection was made at a critical time in Cambodia, considering that tampering incidents comprised the majority of incidents post–1999. While the linkage between incentives and tampering activity is suggested in her work, the relationship is never quantifiably verified. Accordingly, her analysis, which attempts to correlate the intentional engagement with ordnance to a reality of economic incentives, is mere conjecture. My research and quantitative analysis help to further this work.

1.5.3. Keeley (2006)

The primary concentration of the mine action community in Cambodia has been directed at mine clearance. In addition to mine clearance, Mine Action also confronts ordnance issues from perspectives of mine-risk education, stockpile destruction, victim assistance, and advocacy. Funding for these initiatives has never been sufficient and is likely to remain at levels lower than desired by the Mine Action community. Initiatives to combat landmine/UXO issues in Cambodia, while delineated into various projects, were not initially developed from an economic perspective.

Robert Keeley recognized that Mine Action was operating principally outside an economic paradigm. In fact, established prerogatives were put in place that made it difficult to operate according to economic concepts of efficiency. More precisely, the Ottawa Convention allows countries to seek an extension of clearance deadlines but does not allow countries to leave land uncleared, even if the land is of "little or no" economic benefit (Keeley 2006, 294). Mandates to universally clear land ignore financial limitations inherent within mine clearance initiatives and discount the variance of land value that exists. Additionally, this approach ignores the fact that landmines/UXO do not kill people; interaction with ordnance is what kills people.

Keeley investigated the role of various economic tools within Mine Action. Recognizing that resources are limited within Mine Action efforts, Keeley drew from traditional economic theory and subjects these limited resources to economic criteria that seek to maximize efficiency and surplus value. Specific allocation techniques Keeley analyzed involve cost-benefit analysis, multicriteria analysis, linear programming, game theory, and risk analysis. In addition to applying each of these economic tools individually, Keeley made comparisons between the various methodologies in an attempt to maximize results within Mine Action. For example, cost-benefit analysis is compared directly to multicriteria analysis. Analysis takes place within each model and conclusions are reached. Recommendations are made about the allocation of insufficient funds among various Mine Action pillars, land clearance priority determination, and the reconciliation of land values and human life values.

Keeley's work was instrumental in linking Mine Action to economics. Additionally, this work made efforts to distinguish between decisions made on economic grounds alone and endeavors to consider human issues. More exactly, a comment referenced in Keeley's work, made by an unidentified NGO reads as follows: "By looking only at productive land we are reducing the mine problem to a largely economic issue rather than an issue symptomatic of poverty and vulnerability" (317). Accordingly, a concern for the human element of landmine/UXO incidents was indicated in this work.

I rely greatly on the work done by Keeley in linking economic frameworks to Mine Action. While Keeley's work helps to support my research, an important distinction does exist. At the time of Keeley's work, the majority of incidents occurring in Cambodia were accidental in nature. Accordingly, his focus targeted the occurrence of accidents and, therefore, analyzed the economics of removing landmines/UXO from the soil. Tampering incidents now dominate the ordnance problem in Cambodia. More exactly, the majority of landmine/UXO incidents post–1999 have been tampering-specific ones. Therefore, my research steps away from the economics of landmine clearance and attempts to understand the linkage between economic vulnerability, poverty, the price of metal, and tampering incidents. It is my belief that the changing nature of incidents in Cambodia warrants a revisitation of approach.

1.6. HISTORICAL BACKGROUND

An intricate web of political factions contributed to the current landmine and UXO predicament that exists in Cambodia. Official statistics from the CMVIS cite 63,003 in-country landmine-related incident occurrences from January 1, 1979, to December 31, 2007.[6] Landmine/UXO incidents have occurred in every province and district of Cambodia in varying magnitudes. Critical military groups contributing to the current landmine/UXO problem in Cambodia have included US carpet bombers, Royal Government initiatives, the Khmer Rouge, Thailand border protectionists, and the Vietnamese-controlled People's Republic of Kampuchea (PRK). This chapter provides an historical delineation of each ordnance-contributing faction. In addition to demarcating each faction's involvement, this chapter also evaluates the magnitude of ordnance contamination that fell consequent to the faction's involvement and the residual impact of the contamination on Cambodia today.

Section 1.6.1 examines the role US carpet bombers played in plaguing Cambodia with UXO. Section 1.6.2 takes a look at initiatives within the Royal Government of Cambodia, which utilized ordnance. Section 1.6.3 considers the Khmer Rouge and the role it played in increasing landmine-related ordnance in Cambodia. Section 1.6.4 illustrates the impact Thai border protectionists played in complicating ordnance realities. Section 1.6.5 delineates PRK involvement in landmine-related ordnance contamination in Cambodia. In addition to the historical involvement and the consequent quantitative ordnance evaluation, Appendix A provides descriptive narratives for each of the factions described.

1.6.1. US Carpet Bombing

> Blessed are the people whose leaders can look destiny in the eye without flinching but also without attempting to play God.
>
> —Henry Kissinger

Bombing campaigns in Cambodia are inextricably linked to the involvement of the United States in the Vietnam War. North Vietnam, in an effort to bypass the 17th parallel, established alternative and informal travel routes through Laos and Cambodia that became known collectively as the Ho Chi Minh Trail. Soldiers, armament, and supplies traveled south beyond the 17th parallel, reentering Vietnam at numerous places. Travel routes on the infamously illicit trails consisted of a complex network of paths and trails both above and below the earth. Given that there were no clearly traveled trails or paths in the complex network comprising the Ho Chi Minh Trail, efforts by the United States to restrict the surreptitious Viet Cong were complicated at best.

The United States viewed the existence of the Ho Chi Minh Trail as a breach of neutrality on the part of Laos and Cambodia. As a response to covert travel into Cambodia and Laos, Henry Kissinger and President Nixon secretly began a mammoth bombing campaign in both war-neutral countries. Next, in what remains today an act intolerable to many Cambodians, on March 18, 1970, the United States replaced Prime Minister Norodom Sihanouk with Lon Nol, a pro-American political puppet.[7] Lon Nol allowed the bombing of Cambodia to take place and was provided millions of dollars of military and financial support from the United States to build an army against the Khmer Rouge,[8] a Communist guerrilla army forming in the northeast of Cambodia.

In an effort to recapture his rightful throne, King Sihanouk joined forces with the Khmer Rouge. Cambodians still loyal to Norodom Sihanouk subsequently joined the Khmer Rouge en masse. Specifically, official statistics of Khmer Rouge fighters grew from a mere 6,000 before the ousting of King Sihanouk to more than 50,000 within months of him siding with the Communists.[9] Support for the Khmer Rouge continued to grow, eventually leading to a takeover of the country in 1975.

In spite of Lon Nol being imperialist backed and receiving an abundance of western military aid to combat the Khmer Rouge, support for the Communist guerrillas grew at a rate far surpassing that for the Royal Government armies. Millions of Cambodians suffered the wrath of aerial bombardments, a gruesome and bloody reality that left survivors deeply detesting the responsible country. Support for the Khmer Rouge armies grew quickly because they were recognized as directly opposing Western initiatives—specifically, the bombing practices. In addition to attracting those opposing imperialism, the Khmer Rouge continued to grow as Sihanouk loyalists followed him in supporting this initiative. For those who had joined forces with the Khmer Rouge prior to the ousting of King Sihanouk, a renewed fervor invigorated their spirits as they experienced imperialism breaching their domestic borders and killing thousands.

Official records indicate the United States dropped nearly 540,000 tons (1,080,000,000 pounds) of bombs on Cambodian soil.[10] In comparison, a total weight of 160,000 tons of bombs was dropped on Japan during the Second World War. Bombing raids officially comprised 115,273 bomb-drop missions that targeted various locations throughout Cambodia between March 18, 1970, and August 15, 1973. In addition to the officially recognized targets, unofficial carpet-bombing raids erratically released thousands of tons of bombs primarily over eastern Cambodia beginning in 1965 and lasting until early 1975. The magnitude of bombing targets can be observed in Figure 1.1. As is reflected in this map, the majority of US bombing drops occurred on the eastern half of Cambodia.[11]

Calculating the residual UXO that exists in consequence to US carpet bombing is not a simple task. Immediately following the US pullout from Vietnam, financial support was also removed from Cambodia's Royal Armies. Knowing the underbelly of the Royal Army was sliced, the Khmer Rouge seized the capital, Phnom Penh, and gained control of the country. Rates of starvation, rape, murder, disease, and suicide were alarmingly high throughout the Khmer Rouge domination period

FIGURE 1.1. UXO Ordnance Contamination in Cambodia.

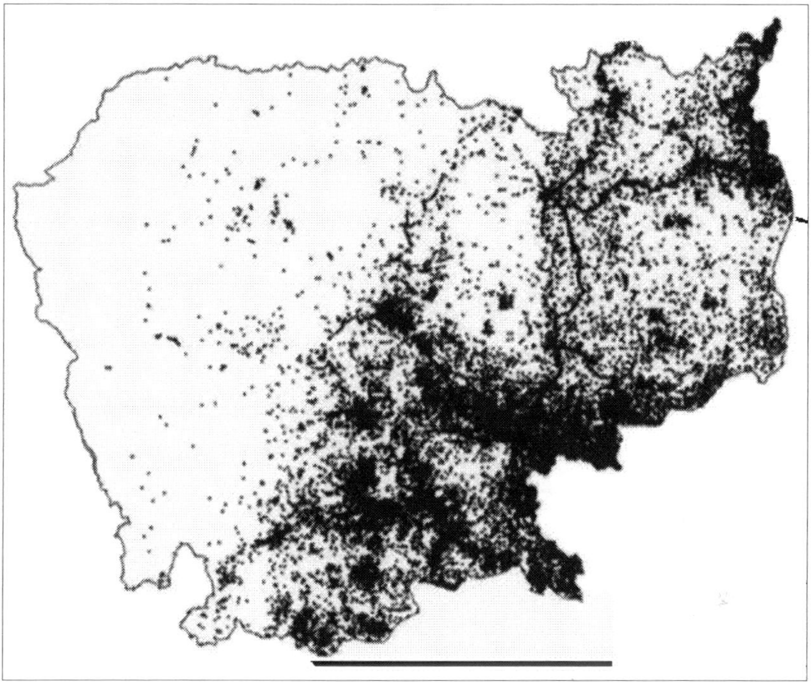

Notes. The United States now admits to 115,273 bombing missions between October 4, 1965 and August 15,1973. The tactical concentration of bombing on the eastern portion of Cambodia is critical to point out for the purpose of later discussion.

(1975–1979). Consequent to the rapid pace at which the Khmer Rouge marched into Phnom Penh following the bombing campaigns, no clear-cut estimation of bombing-related deaths can be separated from the brutality occurring throughout the Khmer Rouge period. Best-guess estimates of civilian deaths related to US bombing campaigns in Cambodia range from 50,000 to more than 1,000,000.

In spite of the abundance of bombing-related deaths, not all of the ordnance dropped on Cambodia exploded on impact. Estimates of ordnance failure rates range from 20% to 60%.[12] Ordnance that fails to explode on initial impact is considered unexploded ordnance (UXO). Reasons for ordnance not exploding include soft soil, landing in water, slowed travel speeds resulting from dense foliage, poor manufacturing design, mistakes made during assembly, water damage, and low drop altitudes. Specific ordnance was actually designed not to explode on impact but rather when shaken or rattled.[13] UXO or dangerous unexploded devices (DUD), as they are commonly referred to in colloquial jargon, remain dangerous despite their harmless appearance. According to failure rate estimates, as much as 324,000 tons (648,000,000 pounds) could have existed in Cambodia beginning in 1975. Postwar interaction with UXO has led to tens of thousands of individuals becoming maimed and killed as a consequence. Accordingly, UXO that originally sat hovering in US war planes continues to pose a threat to those living within Cambodia more than 30 years after it was dropped.[14]

1.6.2. Royal Government Initiatives

> Mines, once laid, are intrinsically different from all other weapons of war because they cannot be recalled by the military when a ceasefire is declared. Each mine must be disarmed, destroyed or claim a victim.
>
> —Rae McGrath[15]

Cambodians have historically viewed both the Vietnamese and Thai through a lens of contempt. Both Thailand and Vietnam are guilty of numerous successful efforts involving stealing land from Cambodia. As bombing raids became commonplace throughout the eastern half of Cambodia, however, a new non-Asian enemy was quickly established. Western powers were seen as authoritative, invasive, controlling, and ultimate indiscriminate executioners.

Left without options, Cambodians fled their home villages. Those not taking refuge with the Khmer Rouge left for provincial capitals and eventually the national capital, Phnom Penh. Cambodians gathered en masse in the heart of their country. Those leaving their bombarded homes expected some degree of assistance and reprieve from family members, friends, and the government. Initially, stockpiles of food were rationed by the government in Phnom Penh. Government analysis, however, quickly revealed the inability to continue rationing food stock at current rates given the reality of increasing populations arriving within the capital. Food was hoarded and rationing practices were halted. Inflation ensued and starvation quickly followed. The bombing continued. This led to continued urban migration flows and increased rates of starvation and death.

The government, headed by Lon Nol, was correctly deemed corrupt and inept at meeting the needs of the people. Corruption continued to escalate at the expense of the starving populace. The Lon Nol administration was despised along with the imperialist supporters backing the government. Support for Norodom Sihanouk increased. A change of government was needed as the well-being of Cambodians hung in the balance of political strife. Prime Minister Norodom Sihanouk joined forces with the Khmer Rouge almost immediately after being ousted in a staged coup. For many Cambodians, trust in the Khmer Rouge was immediate because Sihanouk was initially portrayed as the institutional leader of the organization. The replacement of the Royal Government of Cambodia by the Khmer Rouge on April 17, 1975, was therefore applauded and gratefully accepted. It was believed nothing could be as bad as being ignored by one's own government.

The Royal Government of Cambodia both produced landmines and purchased them from abroad. Cambodia is only known to have produced one variety of landmine, the KN-10. There is no evidence Cambodia has ever exported this landmine,[16] and it can therefore be assumed that all of the KN-10s were used domestically. The 1970s production of KN-10s, a directional fragmentation antipersonnel landmine similar to the Vietnamese MDH-10 and former Soviet Union MON-100, ceased when the Khmer Rouge came to power. No official estimates reflecting the magnitude of KN-10 production exist. The production of KN-10s was, however, likely a small percentage of the armament received internationally.

In addition to the domestic production of the KN-10, the Royal Army of Cambodia received armament from various western powers. The United States admits to the transfer of 622,458 antipersonnel mines to the Royal Government of Cambodia between 1971 and 1975, nearly all of them M18A1 Claymore varieties.[17] Other contributing countries are not as willing to share information about the transfer of landmines to Cambodia's government. Royal Government workers remember receiving approximately 2,000,000 antipersonnel and 6,500 antitank mines from western powers between 1971 and 1975.[18]

Landmines at the disposal of the Royal Government of Cambodia were primarily used to protect provincial capitals and the national capital from encroaching Khmer Rouge forces. It is likely, therefore, that the mines used by the Royal Government are by and large no longer existent.[19] Provincial capitals were eventually all taken by the Khmer Rouge, pushing the surviving inhabitants toward Phnom Penh. Assuming some landmines survived the initial combative efforts of the warring parties, chances are good they also survived the Khmer Rouge domination period. When repatriation efforts were instigated following the fall of the Khmer Rouge, many Cambodians intentionally relocated to the provincial capitals, where food stock and supplies were to be found in greater abundance. Following the ousting of the Khmer Rouge, rapid population increases occurred from rural to urban areas, causing many to undertake informal demining initiatives in order to clear sufficient land to survive. When formal demining agencies came to Cambodia in 1992, they initially concentrated on demining urban centers and high-tourist areas. As evidence of the claim that landmines used by the Royal Government of Cambodia are no longer existent, landmine-related accidents have fallen to a near-zero level in urban centers since 2000.[20]

1.6.3. Khmer Rouge

> I came to carry out a struggle, not to kill people. Even now, and you can look at me, am I a savage person? My conscience is clear.
>
> —Pol Pot, 1997

> The criminal regimes were made not by criminals but by enthusiasts convinced they had discovered the only road to paradise.

> They defended the road so valiantly that they were forced to execute many people. Late it became clear that there was no paradise, that the enthusiasts were therefore murderers.
>
> —Kundera

The Khmer Rouge officially governed Cambodia from April 17, 1975, until being ousted by Vietnamese forces in December 1979. The leader of the Khmer Rouge was Saloth Sar, more commonly known by his alias, Pol Pot.[21] Saloth Sar was born in Prek Sbauv, in the Kampong Thom province, in 1925. At the age of 10, Saloth left his home village to attend a Catholic school in Phnom Penh named École Miche. Because his older sister, Roeung, was serving as a concubine of the then-king of Cambodia, Saloth was afforded access to the royal palace. Many of Saloth's motives to alter government date back to his experience in the royal palace. Saloth qualified for a scholarship at a technical school in France at the age of 24. During his studies in Paris, Saloth became more interested in Communist political meetings than in school, and his grades subsequently suffered. He joined a French Communist Party named Cercle Marxiste in 1951. Saloth eventually was forced to return to Cambodia in 1954 when his grades failed for three consecutive years, making the renewal of his scholarship impossible.

Upon returning to Cambodia, Saloth immersed himself in the study of radically altering government forms by methods of political upheaval, psychological warfare, and coups. During this time, Saloth studied a specific strategic measure of psychological warfare involving the placement of a small patch of landmines near the outskirts of a desired territory, announcing an inflated landmine barrier supposedly surrounding the territory, and intentionally making an example of one of the villagers by forcing him or her to attempt escape through the heavily laid patch of landmines. Saloth made note of this practice, later implementing it on a massive scale. Villages subject to this practice quickly acquiesced to the demands of the Khmer Rouge.

Saloth was the first member of Cercle Marxiste to return to Cambodia and became the leader of the party for Cambodia. In 1962, Tou Samouth, the leader of the Communist movement in Cambodia, was arrested and murdered. Following Tou's murder, Saloth became the next leftist leader of the country. In March of 1963, a list of suspected Communist affiliates, which included Saloth's name, was turned in to King Norodom Sihanouk. Saloth went into hiding near the Cambodia–Vietnam border.

By late 1964, Saloth had persuaded the North Vietnamese to assist in establishing a Cambodian flavor of Communism inside his own country. Financial support and armament were provided to enable the effort. Support of Communist ideals grew rapidly in the northeast of Cambodia. One year after receiving support from the Vietnamese, Saloth met with North Vietnamese leaders in an attempt to receive their support for a Cambodian-led government overthrow. Support was denied because of a previous agreement between Norodom Sihanouk and the North Vietnamese. Specifically, Sihanouk and the North Vietnamese agreed to limit the expansion of a Communist movement within Cambodia in exchange for North Vietnamese passage through Cambodia to assist in its war efforts with South Vietnam. Saloth immediately began establishing plans to break away from the command of the Vietnamese. Importantly, however, Saloth realized current relations feeding the financial pipeline of his movement came from Vietnam. Accordingly, Saloth remained verbally loyal to the Vietnamese brand of Communism while secretly establishing himself as Cambodia's leader.

The first Communist-led attack took place in Cambodia in January of 1968. This attack used armament provided by the Vietnamese in addition to the psychological tactic of landmine fields. It is likely that the use of landmines continued in tandem with small-scale invasions of villages. Savaun Thong, a former Khmer Rouge soldier, remembers following orders to place landmines to the west of his Battambang work camp to dissuade workers from fleeing toward the Thailand border. Those most likely to have encountered a landmine between 1975 and 1979 were those traveling to new locations and those fleeing their work groups. Small-scale attacks against military posts increased in frequency as the strength of the party grew. When an American-backed coup replaced Sihanouk with Lon Nol, the Khmer Rouge changed its strategy to include Sihanouk supporters. The North Vietnamese helped in efforts to recruit Sihanouk and promised an unending supply of armament to combat the newly American-backed country. Having been inaccurately informed of holding a high-standing position in the party, Sihanouk joined the ranks of the Khmer Rouge. Sihanouk addressed the Cambodian people via radio shortly after the coup occurred at a time that the Cambodians were seeking guidance from their former king. Sihanouk instructed the Cambodian people to "rise up against the government and support the Khmer Rouge" (Norodom Sihanouk, a Brief History, 61).

The Vietnamese remained true to their promise and provided armament and fighters to combat the Lon Nol government. Hundreds of thousands of North Vietnamese fighters assisted in ransacking government buildings and establishments. After establishing a strong presence throughout most of Cambodia, the North Vietnamese began withdrawing in 1972. The Khmer Rouge focused its interest on recruitment, especially of the rural classes. With the support of the ousted king and the ever-present bombing campaigns (initiated by capitalists), Cambodians joined the Khmer Rouge in multitudes.[22] Saloth quickly recognized that psychological warfare involved more than landmine manipulation tactics and subsequently used Sihanouk and the US carpet bombing campaign to recruit the vast majority of rural Cambodians.

By 1973, strategic initiatives were in full force to gain control of the capital. The entire Khmer Rouge military power was focused around two military objectives, placing Phnom Penh under siege and purging non-Khmer ethnicities. In regard to placing the capital under siege, access to food from outside Phnom Penh was controlled by the Khmer Rouge. This simplistic mechanism proved as effective as the Khmer Rouge had hoped. In regard to purging non-Khmer ethnicities, the Khmer Rouge systematically exterminated villages comprised of Chinese, Vietnamese, and Cham descendants.[23] Pithy Soen, a newly recruited Khmer Rouge soldier, remembers helping to lay thousands of landmines on the outskirts of a village in the Mondol Kiri province before ransacking the village in the night and forcing the non-Khmer "invaders" across the field; no one survived.

On April 17, 1975, the Khmer Rouge entered Phnom Penh, strongly recognized as the new victors of the country. Internationally, the Khmer

Rouge had already obtained the United Nations (UN) seat, being officially recognized by the 63 UN member countries as the leading party in Cambodia. What was seen as a victory in the first few hours of the Khmer Rouge entering Phnom Penh was soon to become a 4-year nightmare.

The entire population of Phnom Penh was evacuated in a matter of hours.[24] When asked for reasons for the evacuation, the Khmer Rouge responded that it was to avoid the bombing of the capital by the US imperialists. Unfortunately, this excuse was very believable. Cambodians left in all directions, as instructed by the Khmer Rouge, with an initial promise that they would be able to return in 3 days. This promise was far from realistic. Cambodians were placed in work groups around the country. Families were split apart. Money was abolished. Cambodians with western educations were systematically killed. Doctors and teachers were murdered. Death, murder, rape, torture, disease, starvation, and suicide became commonplace. The name of the country was officially changed to Democratic Kampuchea and time was started over, celebrating April 17, 1975, as the beginning of time.[25]

Late in 1976, after having established himself as the ruler of Cambodia, Saloth Sar turned against the Vietnamese and declared them enemies. Border disputes between Cambodia and Vietnam escalated throughout the Khmer Rouge reign of Cambodia until finally, in 1979, more than 100,000 Vietnamese troops were ordered across Cambodia's border to gain control of the country. Vietnam colonized Cambodia for the next 10 years. Pol Pot lived the rest of his life in exile, eventually dying April 15, 1998, in the comfort of his home.

The amount of landmine-related ordnance used by the Khmer Rouge between 1975 and 1979 can only be approximated. In spite of data limitations regarding landmine-specific incidents during this period, information substantiating the supply of armament (including landmines) from both Vietnam and the former Soviet Union is documented at the Ministry of Interior in Phnom Penh. According to these reports, armament was initially provided to the Khmer Rouge from the North Vietnamese armies. After breaking away from Vietnamese control, however, the Khmer Rouge sought and received financial support from the former Soviet

Union. Both Vietnamese and Soviet sources are either not able to or unwilling to provide any estimation of the magnitude of armament provided to the Khmer Rouge forces. Regardless, supporting documentation, in conjunction with the fact that landmines originating from both Vietnam and the former Soviet Union are still discovered in Cambodia's soil, prove the existence and use of landmines originating from these sources.

The NIS in Phnom Penh estimates one in every 380 deaths during the Khmer Rouge domination period occurred consequent to landmine encounters.[26] An approximate estimation of lives lost during this period can therefore assist in determining the magnitude of landmine-related deaths. It should be remembered, however, that landmines were most often used in psychological warfare. It is likely that these landmines served their purpose and are no longer in the ground. Accordingly, the magnitude of landmine-specific casualties can be used to better grasp an historical perspective regarding the use of landmines, the fear Cambodians have of landmines, and the ways in which a genocidal regime used landmines as an instrument. Residual landmines placed by the Khmer Rouge are probably not, however, a problem that survived far beyond the reign of the regime.

Landmine-specific deaths during the Khmer Rouge domination period comprised a finite percentage of the total number of people dying. The majority of Cambodian deaths throughout the Khmer Rouge domination period were a direct result of overwork, starvation, and disease. Those intentionally exterminated were often taken to detention centers, where torture was followed by the filling of mass graves. Several accounts indicate the Khmer Rouge intentionally avoided the use of armament in the extermination of those deemed "enemies to the cause." The most common methods of extermination used throughout the Khmer Rouge period included drowning, burning, live burial, hanging, disembowelment, organ piercing, castration, beatings, waterboarding, scalping, flagellation, oxygen deprivation, dunking, starvation, force-feeding, picquet, suffocation, boiling, electric shock, garroting, mancuerda, rape, body crushing, sleep deprivation, strappado, knife cutting, strangulation, limb crushing, and poisoning. Intentional care was taken to avoid "wasting a bullet" on killing someone.[27] In fact, although guns served as instruments of intimidation, their use against the enemy most often involved swinging the butt of the gun like a club.

Debate regarding the number of Cambodians dying under the Khmer Rouge continues. In spite of ongoing discussion regarding the number of people dying during the Khmer Rouge genocide and the fact that only one in 380 deaths was landmine specific, an approximation of the number of landmines during this time is possible. Estimations of the number of people dying during the Khmer Rouge reign vary from 800,000 to more than 3 million. At the lower end of the spectrum, Khieu Samphan[28] and Saloth Sar state that no more than 800,000 Cambodians died while the Khmer Rouge were in power. The US Department of State calculates 1.2 million deaths during this time. Amnesty International claims a total of 1.4 million died during the same period. The Yale Cambodian Genocide Project estimates a total of 1.7 million deaths. François Ponchaud[29] estimates the death toll between 1975 and 1979 in Cambodia was at 2.3 million. Finally, a figure of 3.1 million was estimated by the People's Republic of Kampuchea. I estimate deaths occurring during the Khmer Rouge reign to be around 2.2 million.

Death toll estimations vary drastically because estimation methodologies are radically different from one another. For political reasons, Khieu Samphan and Saloth Sar claimed a small number of deaths during this time, avoiding any direct or personal connection to them. The US estimations, also low for political reasons, originate from a skull count in mass grave excavations from the early 1990s. Amnesty International and the Yale Cambodian Genocide Project use population growth rate estimations from other countries that undervalue the magnitude of the genocide. François Ponchaud is closest in his estimation, actually using growth rates that existed in Cambodia before and after the genocide and interpolating this data to estimate death tolls. Ponchaud, however, failed to use the 1980 population counts provided by the Vietnamese in his estimations, undercounting the 1980 population by 100,000 and overstating the death count by 100,000. The People's Republic of Kampuchea inflated the death toll to more than 3 million in an effort to pull at the heartstrings of international donors and to convince the Cambodians of the chthonic (demonic) nature of the Khmer Rouge leaders. A summary of the population lost during the Khmer Rouge Genocide is provided in Table 1.1.

Figure 1.2 reflects population figures between 1863 and 2008. Population growth rates were very low between 1863 and 1942. Midway through the 20th century, population growth rates increased, averaging 3.9% between 1959 and 1962.[30] Projecting this growth rate forward gives an estimation of 9.4 million people when the capital fell to the Khmer Rouge in 1975. No census took place in Cambodia between 1962 and 1998. The Vietnamese, however, estimated the population of Cambodia in 1980 at 7.2 million. When a formal population census took place in 1998, it was revealed that Cambodia had 11.4 million people. In order for a population of 7.2 million in 1980 to reach 11.4 million by 1998, an average annual population growth rate of 2.53% was necessary.

Making note of the growth rates of the early 1960s, this figure is not unrealistic. The recent completion of the 2008 General Census of Cambodia discovered a total of 13.4 million, revealing a 1.7% growth rate between 1998 and 2008. The difference between the 1975 population of 9.4 million and the 1980 population of 7.2 million equals

Table 1.1. Estimations of Population Lost During the Khmer Rouge Genocide (1975–1979).

Entity or Author	Population Lost During Genocide
Khieu Samphan & Saloth Sar	800,000
U.S. Dept. of State	1,200,000
Amnesty International	1,400,000
Yale Cambodian Genocide Project	1,700,000
Wade Roberts	2,200,000
François Ponchaud	2,300,000
People's Republic of Kampuchea	3,100,000

Notes. Deaths from landmines during this period only represent 1/380 deaths. In accordance with the range of estimations, landmine incidents during this time range between 2,105 and 8,157. My estimation suggests 5,789 landmine-specific incidents during this time.

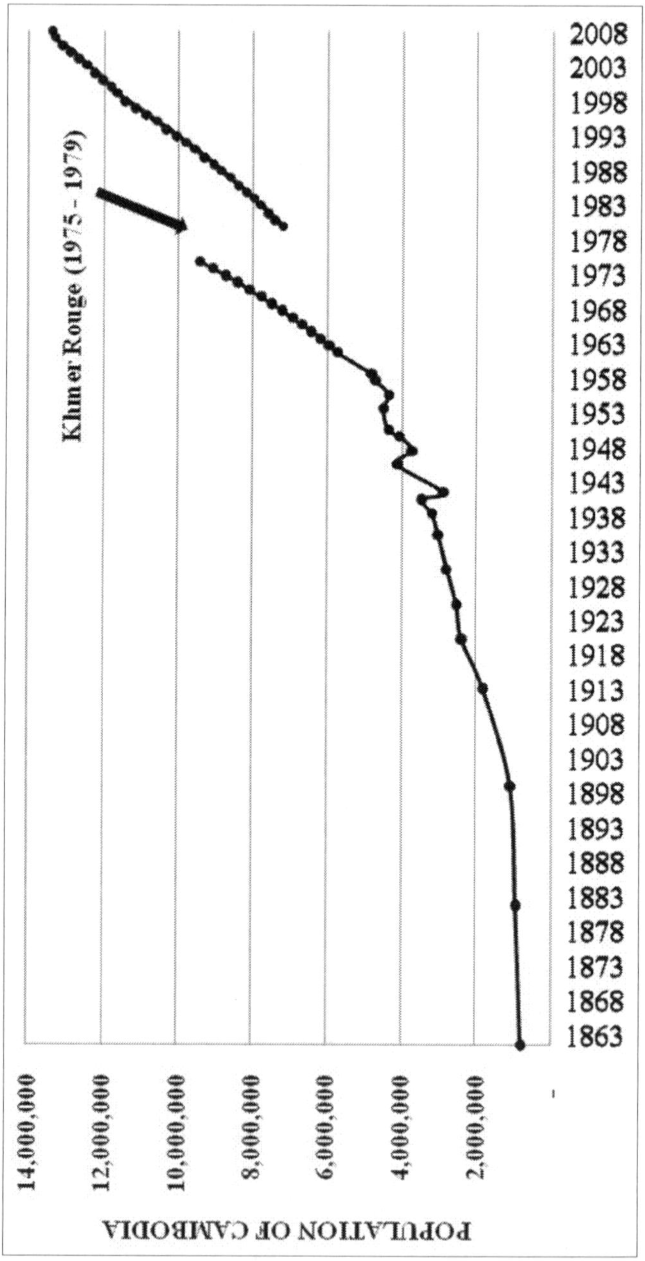

FIGURE 1.2. Population Growth in Cambodia (1863–2008).

2.2 million. While I use this figure to represent the number of people who died during the Khmer Rouge genocide, it should be remembered that time is, in essence, standing still for the period of time being considered. According to my estimation of 2.2 million deaths in conjunction with the stated figure of one in 380 deaths occurring due to landmine-related incidents, 5,789 people died from landmine-specific causes during this period.

1.6.4. Thailand Border Protectionists

> Land mines are the perfect soldiers: they never sleep, and they never die. However, they also don't know which side they're on, or when the war is over.
>
> —Touj Souerly[31]

The border between Cambodia and Thailand has been disputed and disrupted many times throughout these nations' history. The borders between these two countries moved in cadence with the relative strength of each country throughout history. Once, the western border of Cambodia was even pushed east of Angkor Wat, the prominent religious symbol of Cambodia. Territory was bought back by the French protectorate of Cambodia in the 1940s with gold from the towers of Angkor Wat. When Communism was adopted by North Vietnam, Thailand began considering the possibility that Cambodia would eventually follow suit. As the Khmer Rouge began to permeate Cambodia, Thailand border protectionists began securing the border. As Thai border protectionists began laying landmines on the Cambodia–Thailand border in an effort to isolate Thailand from Cambodia and the potential influence of Communism, the strength of Communism grew. Thai officials feared not only the influence of Communism on their current form of government but also the ability of a Communist force to shrink the borders of their country. The border was secured with numerous landmine fields, border fences, and military personnel posted at common crossings. After the Khmer Rouge fell from control of the country, Cambodia was governed by Vietnam. The Thai considered this an even more imminent threat because of the populous nature and military strength of this Communist power. Efforts to secure the border therefore continued throughout the 1979 to 1989 period.

Thailand began using landmines to seal the border between Cambodia and Thailand in 1968 and continued to do so throughout the decade-long Vietnamese occupation of Cambodia (1979–1989). The number of landmines used to secure the border with Cambodia lies between 1,386,883 and 2,669,788.[32] Landmines used to secure the border were both purchased from abroad and produced domestically. Historically, Thailand has produced the Model 123 Claymore-type mine, the U/I TH (AP.1) blast mine, and the U/I TH (AP.2) blast mine.[33] In addition to producing landmines domestically, Thailand is also known to have imported between 427,166 and 499,278 antipersonnel mines from the United States, mostly of the M-18A1 Claymore variety, but also including the M-14 and M-16 landmines, which are known to be banned.[34] In addition to antipersonnel mines produced domestically by Thailand and those received from the United States, other varieties are often found in Thailand's soil. In particular, the PMN-2, POMZ-1, POMZ-2, and Chinese Type 72 have all been found in considerable numbers within Thailand's borders. These varieties are produced in Italy, China, and the former Yugoslavia. It is impossible to know how many of the antipersonnel landmines were placed in Cambodia, defined by the current country borders. The concerns of Thailand in regard to the clearance of landmines stop abruptly at the border. Cambodian landmines, wherever they came from originally, are not considered a concern of Thailand.[35]

According to a survey conducted by the Royal Thai Army,[36] 532 square kilometers of the Cambodia–Thailand border have been deemed contaminated with landmines. Each square kilometer has been identified by the Royal Thai Army as having an average of 3,728 ordnance parcels, totaling 1,983,296 remaining landmines on the border. In a report completed by the U.S. Department of State (Hidden Killers, 1998), an estimated 100,000 landmines were still active along the Cambodia–Thailand border.[37] This area has remained the primary area of concern for landmine-removal efforts until the present day. Accordingly, it can be assumed that whatever the true number of landmines existing in 1998, the number has decreased considerably. A clear separation of responsibility exists along the border in regard to the clearance of ordnance. The Royal Thailand Army accuses the Khmer Rouge and Vietnamese-backed People's Republic of Kampuchea of placing landmines on the Thailand side of the border. The Royal Cambodian Army accuses the Thai military of placing landmines on the Cambodian side of the border. Despite the confusion regarding where the landmines came from, each country only concerns itself with demining efforts on its own side of the current border.

1.6.5. Vietnamese-controlled People's Republic of Kampuchea[38]

Following several small border battles between 1975 and 1978 on the east side of Cambodia, a massive invasion of Vietnamese soldiers pushed past the border on December 22, 1978. Implementing a "blooming lotus"[39] military tactic, the Vietnamese seized operational control of Phnom Penh on January 7, 1979, just 2 weeks after crossing into the country. As the Vietnamese sought to establish control of Cambodia, they did so amid an extreme amount of turmoil and chaos.[40] Eventually ascertaining a degree of political and economic control in Cambodia, the Vietnamese undertook a massive initiative to hermetically seal Cambodia from Thailand. The Vietnamese conscripted hundreds of thousands of Cambodian workers to build an advanced conglomeration of ravines, chasms, fences, and landmine fields, what has proven to be the most extensive minefield in the world.[41] In what became known as the K5 plan, the Vietnamese focused a great degree of attention on sealing off the border from Thailand. By sealing the border, the Vietnamese-backed People's Republic of Kampuchea planned on minimizing the existing threat from the Khmer Rouge while it sought to make Kampuchea a colony of Vietnam.

After the initial ousting of Khmer Rouge from Phnom Penh, Vietnam gained control of the capital. This did not mean, however, that Khmer Rouge armies were obliterated, nor did it mean they were incapable of regrouping. In fact, throughout the decade the Vietnamese controlled Cambodia, between 30,000 and 35,000 Khmer Rouge soldiers existed in the mountainous regions near the border between Cambodia and Thailand.[42] Vietnam proclaimed that if it could secure the border, then protection from outsiders would be certain, while a cleanup action for remaining Khmer Rouge affiliates could easily take place in-country. Battles between the Khmer Rouge and the Vietnamese-backed People's Republic of Kampuchea continued until the latter eventually left Cambodia in 1989. Efforts to build the Southeast Asian version of the Great Wall required the lives of thousands of Cambodians.[43] The ramifications of this protectorate effort are still being felt as men, women, the aged, and the young struggle to build their lives among the minefields.

Vietnam has produced several varieties of antipersonnel landmines. Specifically, Vietnam is known to produce the MBV78A1 fragmentation stake mine, the MBV78A2 can-shaped fragmentation mine, the MN79 plastic blast mine, the MB82B plastic blast mine, the MDH10 Claymore-type directional fragmentation mine, the NOMZ2B fragmentation stake mine, and the P40 "Apple" ball mine. All of these varieties are found during landmine-removal efforts at the Cambodia–Thailand border and were therefore used in the construction of the K5 mine belt.

While no Vietnamese records reflect the number of landmines used in the building of the world's largest mine belt, substantial evidence supports the theory that millions of landmines were placed. Sim Chant,[44] a project manager overseeing the delivery of supplies used on the K5 project in what is now the Svay Chek district located in the Banteay Mean Chey province, attests to hundreds of truckloads filled with mostly landmines being brought to the K5 project. Sim worked as a project manager overseeing the delivery of armament and food supplies to the workers on the K5 project. Sim remembers that there was an abundance of landmines and a shortage of food for the workers. Sometimes the landmines were assembled; other times, the workers were responsible for assembling them before planting them in the ground. Assuming situations were similar in other regions of the K5 mine belt, it is simple to see how millions of landmines could have been used in this massive project.

Determining the number of landmines still in existence near the K5 mine belt is not possible from any existing records or documentation. The number can be approximated, however, by observing average contamination rates among cleared hectares and comparing them to the remaining contaminated land near the Cambodia–Thailand border. Formal agencies cleared a total of 203,263,431 hectares between 2000 and 2005.[45] During these same years, a total of 342,283 antipersonnel mines, 6,847 antitank mines, and 696,877 UXO parcels were discovered and destroyed. This reflects an average annual rate of 174,335 and a total of 1,046,007 ordnance parcels discovered and destroyed during the 6-year span between 2000 and 2005. The majority of these discoveries were made by three dominant landmine-removal agencies in Cambodia: the Cambodian Mine Action Center (CMAC), Hazardous Area Life-Support Organization (HALO), and Mines Advisory Group (MAG).

Given the number of hectares cleared between 2000 and 2006, in addition to the number of ordnance parcels discovered, the average landmine-contamination density per square meters is .005. This means that on average, 195 square meters are cleared for each landmine-related parcel discovered. Put another way, 51.5 ordnance parcels are discovered in the process of clearing an average hectare. While the initial survey of ordnance contamination in Cambodia has largely been discredited due to overcounting and existing discrepancies in measurement methodologies, a more conservative estimate has taken place. Specifically, current landmine surveys estimate 444,600 hectares remain to be cleared of ordnance near the Cambodia–Thailand border. According to the average contamination rates prevalent throughout the past 6 years, it is likely that 22,879,409 ordnance parcels still exist in this region alone.[46] This figure of nearly 23 million trumps the current population of the entire country.

1.7. Human Costs of Contamination

Landmine/UXO incidents in Cambodia have permeated the boundaries of every district, maiming and killing tens of thousands. A total of 58,000 landmine/UXO incidents occurred between 1980 and 2007. Within this figure, 40,189 were civilian incidents. The number of annual incidents has fluctuated drastically, with an extreme high value of 1,814 in 1994 and a low of 347 in 2007.[47] In addition to annual fluctuations, landmine/UXO incidents have also exhibited cyclical behavior in conjunction with dry and wet seasons.

By and large, victims of landmine/UXO incidents are young males. More precisely, males account for 90.6% of all landmine-related incidents,[48] a function of risk-taking behavior. Males undertake risky activities such as tilling suspect soil, traveling in the pursuit of economic gain, and intentional tampering with landmine-related ordnance. Additionally, the 1980 to 2007 mean age of incident occurrence in Cambodia was 31.8 years. While this number speaks of the conglomeration of all 185 districts in Cambodia, district-specific mean age values vary greatly across districts, with a low mean of 9.3 years in the Andoung Meas district and a high of 45.6 years in the Siem Bouk district. Additionally, the mean incident age has been decreasing over time. Specifically, the mean incident age before 2000 was 32.3. This mean value decreased to 26.5 for years following 1999. This finding has important ramifications on postincident survival chances.

Younger demographics are less likely to survive landmine and UXO incidents. More precisely, 48% of landmine-specific and 31% of UXO-specific incidents result in death among those 10 to 19 years of age. This drops to 29% for both groups by the time we reach the 30 to 39 age group because of reduced physical vulnerabilities. Younger persons experiencing the blast of ordnance are more likely to undergo damage to critical organs. Typical landmine design targets the maiming of its victim by concentrating the explosion epicenter in the first three feet nearest to the ground. While this will most likely leave an adult without legs, the first three feet of a child or younger adult often include the groin, stomach and chest areas, and thus the damage is much more severe.

Among those experiencing landmine/UXO incidents in Cambodia, a total of 40,136 among the 58,000 (69.2%) survived their encounters with ordnance. Many landmine/UXO incident victims require years of medical assistance to overcome landmine-related injuries. Typical medical treatments involve blood transfusions, amputations, prosthetic limbs, and years of physical rehabilitation training. In addition to medical assistance, landmine/UXO victims typically require financial assistance with travel expenses, skill-acquisition training, and social support for reintegrating into new atmospheres. The supply of necessary treatments for landmine/UXO victims is limited by funding from international organizations. As of 2008, 11 physical rehabilitation centers and orthopedic workshops existed in Cambodia. Four international organizations operated in the existing rehabilitation centers and workshops. Operational international organizations include International Committee of the Red Cross (ICRC), Cambodia Trust, Handicap International (HI), and Veterans International Cambodia (VIC). Health care workers within these organizations identified challenges such as the lack of blood banks, inadequate trauma care training, and a shortage of ambulance services within the existing medical infrastructure.[49]

The residual ordnance problem in Cambodia is enormous. Initially, as landmine removal efforts commenced, specific attention was given to urban centers, major roadways, hospitals, schools, and the tourist-rich temple regions in Siem Reap. The Royal Government of Cambodia (RGC) established clearing priorities and monitored the success of each operating organization. In addition to managerial tasks, the RGC also contributed to the landmine removal process by providing several clearance teams. The majority of clearance, however, did not take place by RGC teams but rather by the efforts of various other organizations functioning throughout Cambodia.

Organizations functioning in Mine Action throughout Cambodia include the Cambodian Mine Action Center (CMAC), an organization resulting from a United National Development Program (UNDP) project, Mine Advisory Group (MAG), and Hazardous Area Life-Support Organization (HALO). Efforts by mine-clearance teams fluctuate according to funding dollars, technical abilities, and seasonal weather. Funding dollars have recently increased annually, totaling US$30.8 million in 2007.[50] In 2007, funding allowed CMAC to discover and destroy 32,518 antipersonnel mines and 114,755 UXO parcels. HALO shared funding dollars, discovering and destroying 38,912 antipersonnel mines and an additional 10,753 UXO parcels. MAG, the smallest of the landmine-action operators, discovered and destroyed 7,054 antipersonnel mines and an additional 20,425 UXO parcels during the same year. Additionally, RGC discovered and destroyed 219 antipersonnel mines and 13,007 UXO parcels. The aggregate sum between Mine Action organizations includes a total of 78,703 antipersonnel mines discovered and destroyed and an additional 145,344 UXO parcels. International funding dollars, clearance methodologies, and improved technology have all contributed to increased rates of ordnance clearance each year. In spite of this trend, current projections estimate that total clearance of residual landmine/UXO in Cambodia will likely not take place until well into the next century.[51]

In order to sustain a livelihood, more than half the population is primarily engaged in agrarian-related activities. Levels of vulnerability exist among those engaged in agricultural production. Individuals tilling landmine-contaminated fields and foraging for food or wood in unmarked terrain are at a greater risk of encountering ordnance. Individuals left without alternatives to entering the minefields will forage for food inside dangerous boundaries. In addition to agrarian-related incidents, activities specific to traveling and tampering also take place in conjunction with situations of vulnerability. While engagement in any of these activities increases the inherent vulnerability for the individuals involved, the initial conditions preempting involvement with these activities also require a level of risk. As individuals become subject to financial stresses, whether by means of a ceremonial marriage or a disastrous roadside accident, their willingness to engage in risky behavior increases. Vulnerabilities within the areas of agriculture, traveling, and tampering are at the heart of this book and will be examined at length in chapters that follow.

1.8. Combating the Problem

Formal action to combat landmine-related contamination in Cambodia began in 1992.[52] Following established UN guidelines for countries suffering with inordinate amounts of landmine-related contamination, Cambodia adopted the suggested five pillars of mine action: landmine removal, mine-risk education, explosive ordnance disposal, victim assistance, and stockpile destruction. Each of these pillars addresses critical elements associated with the landmine/UXO problem in Cambodia. Decisions regarding the prioritization of pillars differ among the various mine-action affiliates. Each actor within the landmine/UXO community determines the success of its pursuits by comparing year-end accomplishments with predetermined objectives. In exchange for accepting these pillars, Cambodia began receiving international funding to assist with mine-action endeavors.

The current applications of policy regarding the landmine/UXO incident problems in Cambodia do not recognize the relationship between vulnerabilities and the occurrence of incidents. Policy makers should be critically concerned with decreasing the impact on the people of Cambodia by understanding the relationship between specific vulnerabilities and landmine/UXO incidents.

Endnotes

1. Estimates concerning the number of landmine-related parcels existing in each country worldwide place Cambodia at the top of the list in relation to population statistics. Specifically, landmine-to-population ratios in Cambodia are at 1.53. Bosnia and Herzegovina have a ratio of .78, Croatia is at .67, Angola is at .57, Iraq is at .36, Egypt is at .29, Iran is at .24, and Rwanda is at .03. In addition to landmine counts, the existence of UXO dramatically increases the magnitude of residual ordnance parcels.
2. Organizations contributing incident information to CMVIS include the Cambodian Red Cross, hospitals, clinics, the Royal Government of Cambodia, and various other nongovernmental organizations.
3. Countries contributing to landmine/UXO causes in 2008 include Japan, Australia, the United States, the United Kingdom, Canada, the Netherlands, Spain, Finland, Germany, Ireland, Norway, Luxembourg, and New Zealand. Each of these countries contributes to implementing agencies and organizations in dollar values ranging from US$56,000 (New Zealand) to US$6 million (Japan).
4. As of 2007, 84 countries and eight territories continued to suffer from landmine-related impacts.
5. This organization wishes to remain anonymous. The funding used by this organization to implement Bottomley's suggestion comes from discretionary funding, and it is therefore not necessary for this organization to report this practice.
6. CMVIS statistics are housed in Phnom Penh, Cambodia. This study utilizes the complete micro-level dataset of individual-specific information. Summary statistics are available from CMVIS upon request.
7. Lon Nol immediately demanded that the North Vietnamese Army and Viet Cong leave Cambodia. Additionally, Cambodian trade ports were closed to the Vietnamese military troops. Cambodia, traditionally a neutral country, was transformed by Lon Nol's immediate announcement proclaiming a "standing against Communism" similar to his Western supporters.
8. The name *Khmer Rouge* was coined by Prime Minister Norodom Sihanouk. Literally meaning "Red Cambodian" in French, the Communist party in the jungle was most commonly seen wearing black pajamas and red scarves. The term *Khmer Rouge* soon identified the Communist Party of Kampuchea (CPK), the Party of Democratic Kampuchea, the Khmer Communist Party, and the National Army of Democratic Kampuchea. The term now stands as

a constant reminder of a life of repression, mass extermination, and starvation that existed while Cambodia was governed by the Khmer Rouge (1975–1979).

9. Norodom Sihanouk, a Brief History, p. 32.
10. The actual recorded tonnage amounts to 539,129 tons, 257,465 of which were dropped during the last 6 months of bombing raids.
11. This point becomes critical in future chapters when making observations that the majority of UXO incidents occur in the west.
12. Interview between author and CMAA Deputy Secretary General, Leng Sochea, April 2007.
13. International Campaign to Ban Landmines, Landmine Monitor Report: 1999 – Cambodia.
14. Between 1979 and 2007, a total of 12,804 UXO-specific incidents have been recorded by CMVIS in Cambodia.
15. Quote from *Landmines: A Legacy of Conflict; a Manual for Development Workers* (McGrath, 2004).
16. United Nations, 2005.
17. United Nations, 1999.
18. Information obtained by author in an interview with Choeun Pon in April 2007. Choeun was a commander in charge of accounting for supplies during the war.
19. The prevalence of incident occurrence in provincial heads is almost non-existent. Urban areas that did have contamination after the war were given priority of clearance.
20. Although landmine-related "accidents" are at a near-zero level in Cambodia as of 2000, tampering continues to exist throughout Cambodia in both urban and rural areas. Tampering, however, involves the movement of metal and one should not, therefore, presume that incident locations are identical to initial locations of ordnance.
21. The name Pol Pot came from "pol*itique* pot*entielle,*" a phrase coined for Saloth Sar by Chinese government officials. *Politique potentielle* translates from French to mean "the potential of politics."
22. By 1973, it is estimated that the Khmer Rouge controlled 60% of the country and more than half the population.
23. The initial purging of minority groups in Cambodia served as a testing ground for Saloth Sar in regard to methods of torture and extermination. These tactics would soon be used on the educated elite inside the country.
24. The evacuation of urban areas was not new to the Khmer Rouge, but it had never been carried out at the level of the evacuation of Phnom Penh.

The Khmer Rouge first evacuated the entire population of Ratanakiri in 1968 in order to better control the population. Some cities were evacuated because of the inability to stop engaging in capitalistic behavior. Phnom Penh was evacuated primarily to use the people in agrarian labor and to completely eradicate any traces of capitalism in Cambodia.

25. *Year Zero* was the specific term used by the Khmer Rouge to denote the significance of the event.
26. The National Institute of Statistics has gathered data regarding Khmer Rouge genocidal tactics. The institute estimates the proportion of genocidal victims that were subject to starvation, torture, landmines, and disease as causes of death. Estimations are based on hundreds of thousands of reports gathered from villages around Cambodia.
27. Information obtained by author in an interview with Phath Chhen, a survivor of the Khmer Rouge genocide, November 2000.
28. Khieu Samphan served as President of Democratic Kampuchea throughout the reign of the Khmer Rouge. Effectively, Khieu Samphan was the head of state in Cambodia, although Saloth Sar remained in control.
29. The author of "Cambodia: Year Zero".
30. Population statistics prior to 1959 were obtained in the French Census Tables of Cambodia entitled "L'evolution demographique du cambodge dupuis l'origine au recensement en 1962."
31. Chief of Veal Thom in Cambodia. Touj Souerly had an encounter with a landmine in 1998.
32. After more than a decade of placing landmines at the Cambodia–Thailand border, a massive landmine removal effort has led to the eradication of numerous mines. Based on current discovery ratios of the varying antipersonnel landmine varieties, between 12% and 27% of landmines discovered are of the M-18A1variety. In light of this observation and knowledge of the number of M-18A1 landmines imported from the United States, we can estimate the total number of landmines used in Thailand at between 1,849,178 and 3,559,717. Additionally, three-fourths of the total landmine-related incidents occurring in Thailand occur on the Cambodia–Thailand border. Accordingly, it is safe to assume that between 1,386,883 and 2,669,788 antipersonnel landmines were used to secure the border.
33. Letter from US Army Foreign Science and Technology Center to Human Rights Watch, 1 November 1993, p. 1; US Department of State, Outgoing Telegram, Unclassified, Subject: landmine export moratorium demarche, 7 December 1993.

34. United States Army, Armament, Munitions, and Chemical Command (USAMCCOM), Letter to Human Rights Watch, 25 August 1993, and attached statistical tables, provided under the Freedom of Information Act. (No page number). This document gives the exact number and type of mines shipped each year from 1969–1992.
35. Mine-clearance initiatives started in 1985.
36. Survey performed in 1998.
37. United States Department of State, *Hidden Killers: The Global Landmine Crisis,* September 1998, p. A-2.
38. The term *Kampuchea* is typically used to denote Cambodia before 1993. On the June 29 in this year, Cambodia officially changed its name from Kampuchea to Cambodia.
39. The "blooming lotus" military strategy operates around an idea of quickly gaining control of the center of the country (in this case Phnom Penh) and then opening a range of control in concentric circles around the initial area of control. This tactic was no doubt named for the similar way in which a lotus flower blooms.
40. This is elaborated upon in Chapter 2 in discussion about the K5 Era.
41. More specific details are provided in Chapter 2 in relation to the K5 Era.
42. Slocomb, M. (2001). K-5 gamble. *Journal of Southeast Asian Studies*, *32*(2), 195.
43. Information obtained by author in various interviews with individuals formally involved with K5 projects.
44. Interview with Sim Chant by Author in April, 2007. Many other K5 engineers have also attested to these findings.
45. Information compiled from *Landmine Monitor Reports 2000, 2001, 2002, 2003, 2004,* and *2005* (International Campaign to Ban Landmines).
46. The density of landmine contamination along the K5 mine belt is fairly evenly distributed. When K5 projects commenced, units were stationed every few kilometers and tasked with similar objectives. The supply of landmines was universal among all units. No evidence exists, therefore, substantiating that areas remaining to be cleared are less densely contaminated.
47. The high and low estimates consider only the civilian-specific incidents.
48. Of the 5,837 female-specific incidents occurring between 1980 and 2008, only 237 were military specific.
49. The majority of NGO enterprises treating landmine/UXO victims are urban based and require victims to travel to urban centers before treatment can commence.

50. According to *Landmine Monitor Report 2005* (International Campaign to Ban Landmines), 14 countries (including the European Commission) contributed $30,797,541 to mine action in Cambodia in 2007. This monetary figure represents a 4% increase compared to 2006 ($29.6 million). In spite of increased funding, funding at the 2007 level does not appear sufficient to meet all of Cambodia's substantial mine action needs. As of July 2008, the United Nations Mine Action Service (UNMAS) noted "insufficient funding compared to the scope of contamination" as a primary factor impeding mine action in Cambodia.
51. The initial Ottawa Convention deadline of 2012 has been deemed impossible to meet. Convention extensions are currently being prepared. CMAA Deputy Secretary General H. E. Leng Sochea calculates that at the current trend of clearance, it will require more than 100 years to meet the stipulations of the convention.
52. Formal action involves the action of trained and internationally approved demining action. Informal action has existed, and will continue to exist, whenever a demand for demining exists and formal sectors do not immediately satisfy this demand. Prior to 1992, only informal means of demining existed in Cambodia. Although this is now an illegal action, punishable by fines and imprisonment, it nonetheless still takes place.

CHAPTER 2

LANDMINE/UXO-RELATED INCIDENTS IN CAMBODIA

1980–2007

All things appear and disappear because of the concurrence of causes and conditions. Nothing ever exists entirely alone; everything is in relation to everything else.

—Buddha

2.1. INTRODUCTION

In this chapter, I first distinguish among three types of landmine and UXO-related incidents and provide a description of their relative magnitudes and geographic distribution between 1980 and 2007. Second, I give a detailed account of economic and historical factors lying behind these incidents as a backdrop to the statistical analysis occurring in the next three chapters.

Landmine/UXO incidents involve the combination of accidents and tampering episodes and result in maiming, amputation, and death. Landmine/UXO incidents in Cambodia have been tracked since 1980 by a myriad of national and international organizations including hospitals, health centers, governmental organizations, and several nongovernmental organizations (NGOs).[1] Landmine and UXO incidents are initially recorded at a local level and then reported to the Cambodian Mine/UXO Victim Information System (CMVIS) in Phnom Penh. CMVIS compiles records into a central database, publishing monthly casualty reports and annual trend statements for the Cambodian Mine Action Authority (CMAA), the delegated mine-action authority of the Royal Government of Cambodia. Compilations of data at CMAA are then utilized in producing progress reports for current and prospective donors worldwide.[2] CMVIS datasets categorize landmine/UXO victims according to age, sex, military or civilian status, incident location (province, district, commune, and village), participating incident activity (farming, tampering, etc.), incident type (maiming or death), landmine/UXO incident distinctions, incident terrain, mine-risk education status, and date of incident.[3]

According to the CMVIS data, between 1980 and 2007, 40,189 civilians suffered the direct impacts of landmine-related incidents in Cambodia. This figure ranged from an annual high of 1,814 in 1994 to a low of 347 in 2007.[4] On average, 1,488 landmine-related incidents have occurred annually in the observed period. Figure 2.1 displays the annual nonmilitary landmine/UXO incidents in Cambodia between 1980 and 2007. This figure shows that while the number of incidents fluctuated substantially over time, the levels declined and stabilized after the late 1990s.

In an effort to understand the nature of incidents each year, Figure 2.2 distinguishes between incidents specific to agrarian, travel, and tampering activities. Agrarian-related incidents may take place during burning, being a bystander, clearing, cutting, collecting, construction, farming, herding, labor, playing, and toileting. The traveling category excludes UXO-related travel incidents owing to the fact that these are likely a result of tampering. Tampering is specific to the intentional handling of landmines and UXO, including their use in fishing and transportation.

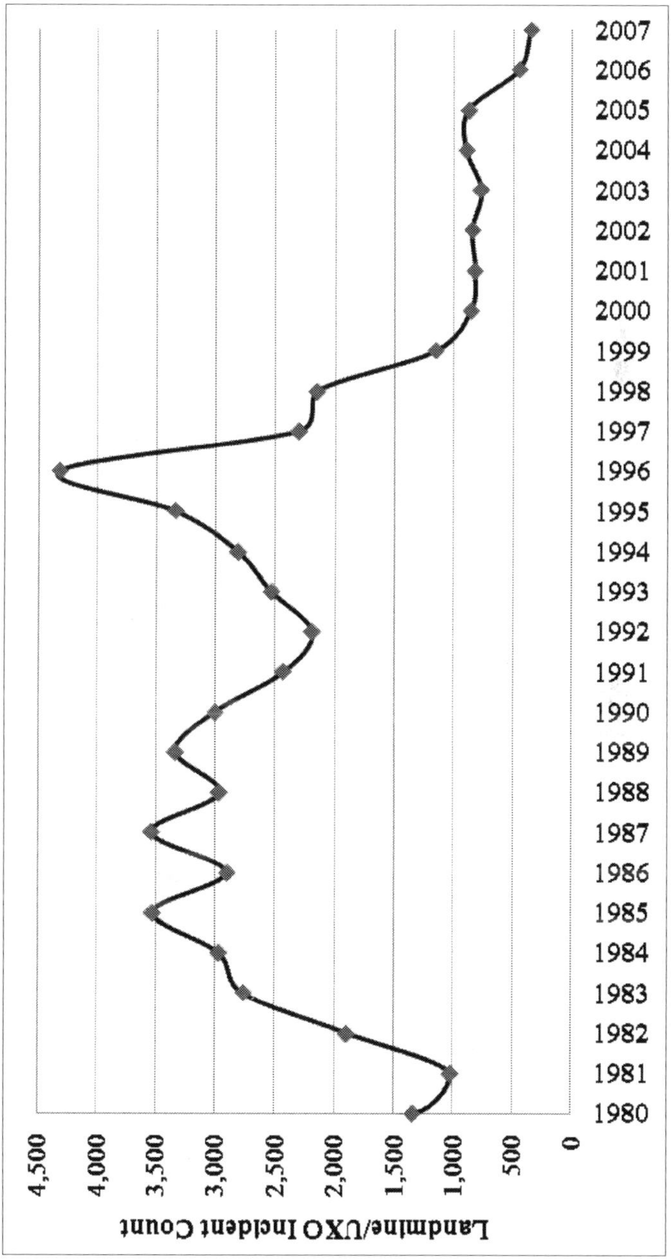

FIGURE 2.1. Annual Landmine/UXO Incidents in Cambodia (1980–2007).

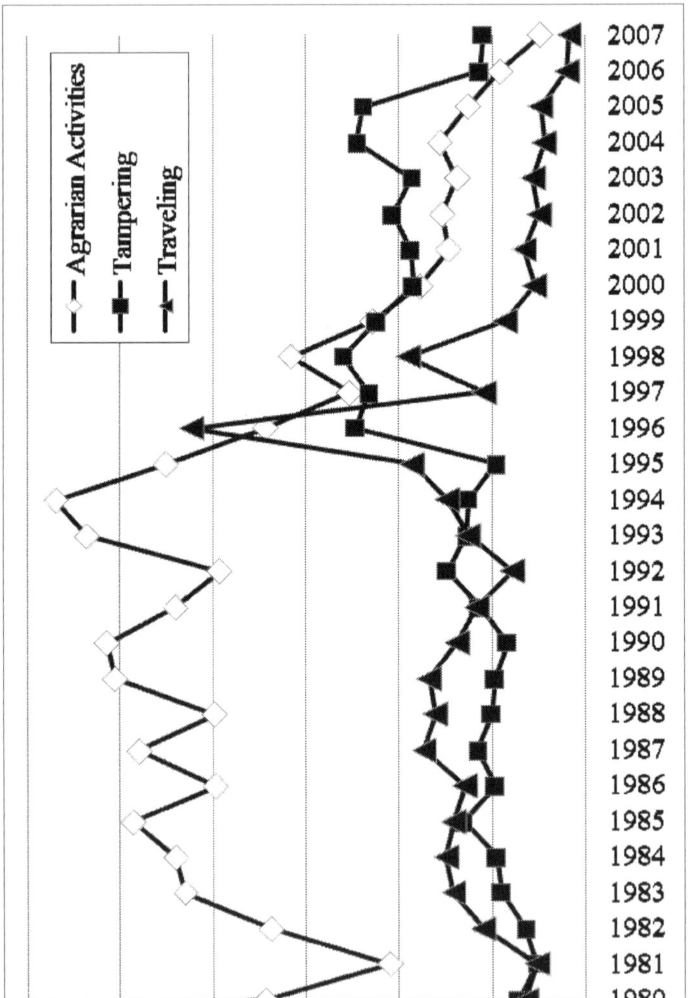

FIGURE 2.2. Landmine/UXO Incidents by Category (1980–2007).

The current definition of tampering used by the Mine Action community only includes overt admissions of handling ordnance. This work redefines tampering in a framework that captures economic incentive structures as explored and explained in Chapter 5.

Most of the incidents occurring before 2000 were specific to agriculture, and the drop in total incidents after 1998 is attributable primarily to the decline of this type of incident. Travel-related incidents were relatively steady throughout the period except for the sharp increase in 1996, but they also declined after 1998. By contrast, tampering-related incidents increased after 1995 and even exceeded the agrarian activity-related incidents. Tampering incidents are now the dominant type of incident occurring in Cambodia.

Geographic distribution of each type of incident at the district level is illustrated in Figure 2.3.[5] A summary table of the geographic characteristics related to landmine/UXO incidents in Cambodia is provided in Table 2.1. This table lists the high-impact districts, means, maximums, and minimum values. Additionally, this table lists the Moran's I calculations concerning spatial autocorrelation for each of the observed incident activities.[6] The Moran's I values within each of the economic categories of distinction reflect a value significantly higher than the minimum value necessary to establish positive spatial autocorrelation.[7] Figure 2.3 and associated statistics indicate that all three types of incidents were concentrated in the northwestern districts.

The following three sections of this chapter examine in greater detail agrarian-, travel-, and tampering-related incidents with emphasis on their economic and historical background.

2.2. Agrarian-specific Landmine/UXO Incidents

The working hypothesis of this section is that landmine-related incidents are inversely related to the level of rice production. More specifically, landmine-related incidents decrease once a sufficient amount of rice is available. When people do not possess sufficient food to meet their needs, they are often forced to engage in activities that increase the

FIGURE 2.3. District Prevalence of Landmine/UXO Incidents in Cambodia by Economic Activity (1980–2007).

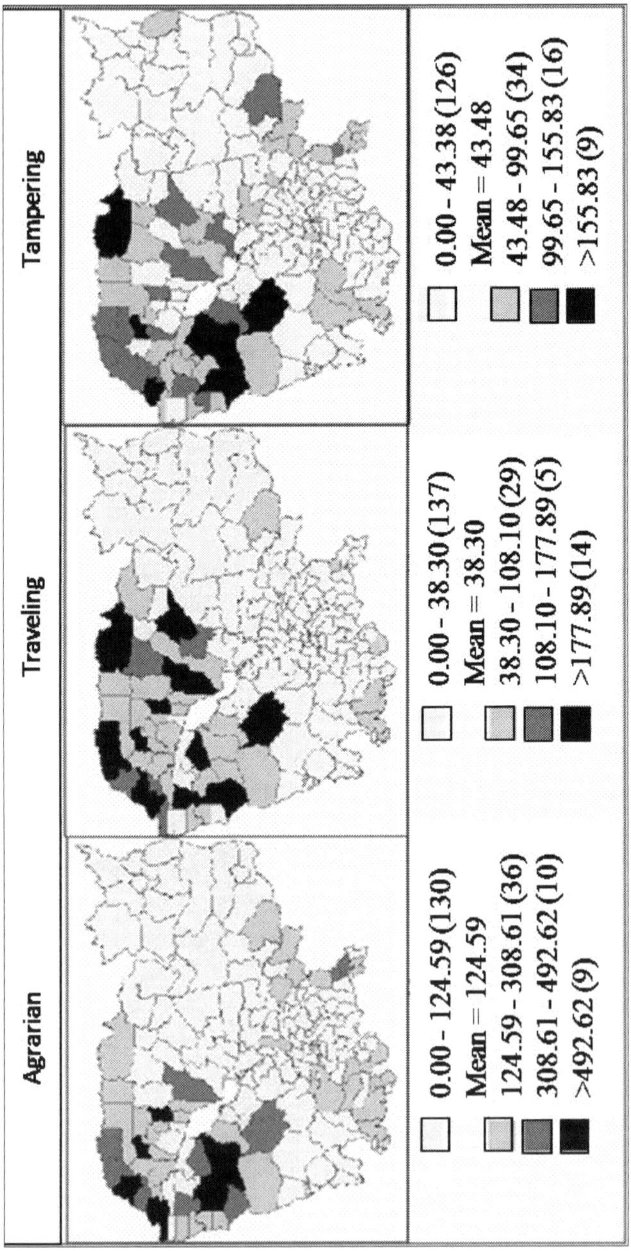

Table 2.1. Landmine/UXO High-Impact Districts in Cambodia.*

	Agrarian	Travel	Tampering
Mean District Incident Occurrence	124.59	38.3	43.48
Maximum District Value	1,252	492	268
Minimum District Value	0	0	0
High-Impact Districts**	On Chrov, Malai, Thma Puok, Battambang, Moung Ruesei, Srei Snam, Rotonak Mondol, Banan, Banteay Srei	On Chrov, Battambang, Phnum Kravanh, Choam Khsant, Svay Chek, Srei Snam, Sangkae, Samlout, Rotonak Mondol, Banteay Ampil, Banteay Srei, Rovieng, Samraong Tong, Bavel, Chi Kraeng	On Chrov, Battambang, Phnum Kravanh, Choam Khsant, Moung Ruesei, Srei Snam, Sangkae, Samlout, Rotonak Mondol
High-Impact Value	>492.62	>177.89	>155.83
Moran's I	0.4171	0.3912	0.479

Note. *Values per population of 10,000. **High-impact districts include those at least 3 standard deviations greater than the mean.

likelihood of encountering landmines. This section provides an historical perspective to agriculture in Cambodia by considering impediments to agricultural production and distribution.

Section 2.2.1 considers landmine-related incidents in conjunction with rice production levels by specifically looking at the history of planting intensities, varieties of rice planted, usage of fertilizers, irrigation control, and natural disasters. Section 2.2.2 takes a look at stated rice production levels and describes domestic distribution problems and Vietnamese pilfering practices.

2.2.1. Rice Production

In January 1979, the People's Republic of Kampuchea (PRK), a Vietnamese-installed government, officially replaced the Khmer Rouge. Rice was nearly nonexistent when the Khmer Rouge armies were in power, was not sufficient during the PRK domination period, and is still not being produced and distributed to a degree that adequately combats chronic food insecurity or high rates of malnourishment. The amount of rice available for consumption in Cambodia has varied drastically from season to season, reflecting the greatest degree of variance between 1980 and 1996. In line with the great degree of agricultural vulnerability, agriculture-specific landmine-related incidents dominated the incident count during most of this period.

During the Khmer Rouge domination period (1975–1979), families were uprooted, family farms were replaced with collective farm initiatives, irrigation channels were destroyed, and produce yields were centrally controlled. Cambodians surviving the Khmer Rouge were on the brink of succumbing to starvation. When the Vietnamese invaded Cambodia in December of 1978, obtaining food was a priority of the utmost importance. In an effort to recover from extreme malnourishment, millions wandered the landscape in search of food. Temporary relief was found by many as rice storehouses were stormed, and 66% of the country's stock of buffalo, pigs, and cows was slaughtered (Gottesman, 2003).[8] This relief was only temporary, however. Cambodians were in desperate need of food stocks amid the chaotic government overthrow.

Following the Vietnamese invasion of Cambodia, the United Nations Children's Fund (UNICEF) and World Food Program (WFP) engaged in a massive food relief effort established near the Cambodia–Thailand border. A massive "land bridge" of sorts was created whereby Cambodians could cross the border to Thailand for food supplies and then return to Cambodia (Asia Watch: Physicians for Human Rights [AWPHR], 1991). As a result of food flights to Thailand and provincial capitals, more than 30% of the country's rice fields were left fallow (Gottesman, 2003).[9] The combination of fallow crops, absent seed stock, and sparse animal supplies constituted a food crisis that continued to fill the mass graves of the country.

By April of 1979, after experiencing aborted dry-season harvests and losing rice seed to spring planting, the supply of food was well below the needs of the country. Nearly 100,000 Cambodians had reached the Cambodia–Thailand border by June 1979 in an effort to receive reprieve. This action decreased farm production and harvest yields in the next season. In addition to the decreased ability to produce food in the next period, a simultaneous influx of more than 200,000 Vietnamese soldiers placed an increased strain on the domestic supplies of rice (Brown & Zasloff, 1998).[10]

The intensity with which rice was planted, cultivated, and harvested in Cambodia varied drastically for years following the collapse of the Khmer Rouge. The combination of displaced families, emergency food aid being provided at the border, and the absence of traditional irrigation control mechanisms led to a great degree of variance concerning rice planting across the country. On average, hectares planted increased throughout the period—except for the years 1984 to 1987 following a Vietnamese initiative to hermetically seal the Cambodia–Thailand border that began in 1984. This effort, known as the "fifth plan" (K5), used millions of landmines and hundreds of thousands of laborers and ultimately reduced rice planting and the production of rice.

Rice production can be increased by cultivating higher-yield varieties, increasing the use of fertilizers, and implementing flood-control irrigation practices. In addition to these variables, the production of rice is largely contingent on its growing to maturity. Despite the use of high-yield rice varieties, fertilizers, and flood-control irrigation mechanisms, a portion of each year's crop is lost to natural disasters in the form of floods, droughts, and insect infestation.

Cambodian farmers were accustomed to planting low-yield rice varieties and were reluctant to switch to higher-yield varieties, even when stock was provided free of charge from international donations, due to the lack of irrigation sources and the increased risk of producing a yield with a volatile supply of water. Typically, low-yield rice varieties grow in a range of water depths, and their output is less dependent on variations in rain volume. High-yield rice varieties, however, come at an increased risk of failing when not grown in a specific range of water depths. Currently, irrigation flood-control mechanisms exist for only 20% of rice fields. Therefore, farmers often opt to plant lower-yield rice seed with the certainty that a yield will be produced rather than plant higher-yield varieties with a strong possibility of losing the entire crop. The use of higher-yield varieties is, therefore, contingent on an in-place system of irrigation.[11]

The use of fertilizers can also prove very effective in increasing rice yields. When fertilizers were provided, farmers throughout Cambodia saw radically increasing rates of rice yields, which allowed them to save seed stock and gradually convert toward using higher-yield rice varieties. This allowed farmers to spend time developing irrigation infrastructures, expanding their future planting options. Fertilizers are expensive to produce and difficult to transport, making the subsidization of seed stock a more appealing option than fertilizers for international donors. When fertilizers are provided, however, farming options are quickly expanded and taken advantage of. Fertilizers bring nutrients to arid, desiccated soil and increase the yield of crops whether farmers plant low- or high-yield seed varieties. Whereas the use of high-yield seed varieties has the potential to multiply the crop yield by a factor of 5 in some cases, it comes with a degree of risk wherein the crop may completely fail. The use of fertilizers, while not able to produce quantities like high-yield varieties, still do increase crop yields. It therefore follows that farmers in every conceivable situation would opt to use fertilizers if offered in the form of a subsidy.

Perhaps the most critical factor in determining the production of rice is water. The supply of water to rice fields can be accomplished by means of rain, irrigation, or spillover from the Tonle Sap lake/river system.[12] The flood plains of Cambodia are naturally suited for growing rice. As the Tonle Sap expands each rainy season to three times its dry-season size, 27% of the country's rice fields are naturally flooded. The remaining rice fields, too far from the Tonle Sap, rely on a sufficient supply of rain to produce a harvest. Irrigation channels, once abundant throughout Cambodia's landscape, were destroyed by the Khmer Rouge in an ironic attempt to return to an agrarian state. Remaining channels are primarily located in areas that receive spillover from the Tonle Sap. The absence of irrigation from the remainder of the country is a critical limit to the use of higher-yield rice varieties and the production of rice during the dry season.

Crops are often subject to natural disasters in the form of droughts, floods, and insect infestation. When water levels are not controlled, floods and droughts can completely destroy a crop. Insect infestation can be avoided by using pesticides, which can prove quite costly for farmers to purchase. The areas of Cambodia most susceptible to crop loss due to natural calamities are those lacking irrigation channels that would control water levels. Without this control mechanism, farmers lose their crops to early flooding, late flooding, excess rains, dry spells, and many other phenomena.

Ultimately, the combination of high-yield rice varieties, the use of fertilizers, and controlling water depths with irrigation mechanisms provides the best chance of producing agricultural yields while at the same time avoiding the wrath of nature.

2.2.2. Distribution of Rice

The net quantity of rice produced in Cambodia is not the end of the story. One important caveat to consider is how effectively rice is distributed. Distribution of rice was the prerogative of the Vietnamese soldiers throughout Cambodia, who often appropriated a substantial portion of rice for themselves before distributing the remaining stock. It was also common during the 10-year occupation of Cambodia by Vietnam for authority figures in charge of the distribution of rice to sell provisions to Thailand or Laos for a price even beneath a domestic production cost. Because the provincial heads were autonomous, self-governing agents of the political regime, they were in charge of reporting production levels and more often than not appropriated a hefty portion for themselves. This political structure ensured food distribution problems while at the same time protecting the provincial authority from being implicated in illegal trade or extortion.

Rice farmers were instructed that they would receive food stock in accordance with their own production, but the distribution of rice from PRK leaders to civilians rarely took place, leading to black markets and efforts to hide rice from the authorities.[13] While sufficient food stock was being produced domestically to meet the caloric needs of Cambodians, starvation was rampant.

When hundreds of thousands of Cambodians were conscripted to work on the K5 mine belt, many fields were left fallow.[14] In the following seasons, rice production decreased dramatically. People began to hoard rice. Hoarders bribed the officials and made inaccurate statements about natural disasters. At any rate, the distribution of rice cannot be assumed to take place evenly. Individuals not involved in the rice-production process were at a distinct disadvantage.[15]

In addition to problems regarding the domestic distribution of rice, substantial evidence indicates that much of the rice produced in Cambodia was extracted by the Vietnamese occupiers. Throughout the entire decade of Vietnamese occupation, Vietnam was struggling to produce enough rice to meet its own domestic demand. As a new protectorate of Cambodia, PRK forces justified pilfering rice to alleviate their domestic rice shortage problems. Existing government reports reflect more than 41,000 tons of rice sent to Vietnam during 1981 alone (Gottesman, 2003). This practice continued in the next decade.[16] Meeting the caloric needs of the civilian population, therefore, was a function of the production of rice and Vietnamese seizure of rice, ostensibly in return for providing Cambodia with a functioning army.

2.3. Traveling-specific Landmine-related Incidents

Following the overthrow of the Khmer Rouge, travel in Cambodia was chaotic. However, several factors in post–Khmer Rouge Cambodia led to massive movements of population in spite of the widespread danger of encountering landmine-related ordnance. Immediately following the Vietnamese invasion of Cambodia, millions of Cambodians began the search process to find lost family members. This required travel toward hometowns and, for many, a search for orphans near the Cambodia–Vietnam border. Many sought relief in urban centers or across international borders. Later, under the direction of the Vietnamese, hundreds of thousands of Cambodians were uprooted and forcibly conscripted to join K5 projects. Those seeking aid in Thailand eventually crossed back into Cambodia, either voluntarily or because of forcible repatriation mandates. Additionally, years after the establishment of Cambodia as a sovereign power, property rights were radically altered, dramatically influencing rates of travel across Cambodia. These factors directly expanded travel in Cambodia and predisposed people to travel-related landmine incidents. A total of 6,913 travel-specific landmine-related incidents took place in Cambodia between 1980 and 2007, accounting for 18% of the total incidents. As shown in Figure 2.2, the total number of travel-specific incidents rose sharply around 1996, but otherwise, they account for a relatively stable number of incidents, with a declining trend after the late 1990s.

The remainder of this section is organized as follows: Section 2.3.1 explains the family-search processes that commenced following the ousting of the Khmer Rouge and continued for several years. Section 2.3.2 elaborates on travel taking place to provincial centers and across international borders. Section 2.3.3 considers several compulsory initiatives related to travel that took place under the control of the Vietnamese-backed government between 1979 and 1989. Section 2.3.4 discusses the travel-related ramifications of the change of property rights.

2.3.1. Family-related Travel

Efforts to reunite families commenced immediately following the invasion of Vietnamese forces in December of 1978. Uncertainty about the whereabouts of family members led many toward hometowns in hopes that other family members would undertake similar actions. While no official registry existed concerning the whereabouts of any specific individuals, word quickly spread across Cambodia that surviving orphans were being shipped in multitudes to specific holding centers in Vietnam. Many Cambodians traveled to Vietnam in hopes of finding their lost children.[17] Complicating travel endeavors was a simultaneous effort by the Vietnamese to repopulate Cambodia with those who had fled the Khmer Rouge regime (Martin, 1989).

The presence of immediate family was required in order to get orphans released from holding centers in spite of the difficulty of providing proof of identity or birth certificates. This led some to attempt traveling to their initial place of residence in hope of finding documentation, while others traveled to acquire anything that could be used to purchase back their children from the Vietnamese.[18] Complicating the issue further was the vague definition of what constituted an "orphan" within border camps along the Cambodia–Thailand border. Sometimes children being cared for by aunts and uncles were considered orphans and taken to Vietnam, whereas grandparents typically constituted an adequate guardianship claim. The specific age at which an individual was considered an adult was also a critical area of confusion. Single females as old as 24 were often transported as orphans, whereas males were often considered independent adults at ages as young as 12. Confusion resulting from this inconsistent process influenced repeat travel for a considerable amount of the population. Journeys were taken on foot and almost always lasted for months.

As orphans were finally released from holding centers in February 1981, the proportion of travel-specific landmine incidents rose drastically among the young. In 1980, the 5 to 14 age group represented 14.4% of landmine-related incidents. According to the CMVIS dataset, this number grew to more than 22% by 1981.[19] Many of the released orphans were not left in the care of legal guardians but were instead released in the loosest sense of the term. Many orphans found foster family structures within the provinces of Svay Rieng, Kampong Cham, and Prey Veaeng, all along the Cambodia–Vietnam border. Many of the adopted orphans in the Svay Rieng province undertook traditional age-specific herding activities, causing a dramatic increase in landmine/UXO incidents for several years following the termination of Vietnamese-sponsored orphan programs.

Further obscuring efforts to reunite families in the years following the invasion of the Vietnamese was the inability of the population to travel on traditional roads. In an effort to stabilize the Cambodian economy, the Vietnamese stationed military units at several critical road junctions and required travel documents from the Cambodians. Permission was only granted when travel documents contained the numerous requisite signatures or bribes were paid. This restriction forced many to undertake travel across more treacherous terrain, which led many to experience unfortunate encounters with landmines and UXO.

2.3.2. Relief Travel

Devastating outcomes seemed inevitable both for Cambodians migrating toward provincial centers or hometowns and for those who were attempting border crossings. Millions of Cambodians wandered the landscape of their war-torn country, primarily in search of family or food, with outcomes that were at best ambiguous. As bureaucratic structures were struggling to rebuild in an atmosphere of corruption, Cambodians made decisions about relocating according to the available information at hand, which typically included nothing more than word of mouth from passing strangers. Several conflicting incentive structures existed, causing some to flee westward while others were urged to go east.

Following the arrival of the Vietnamese in early 1979, many Cambodians took immediate action and fled to Thailand, an area considered safe. Landmine/UXO encounters were inevitable with increased travel across the dangerous K5 minefields, but those surviving the trip explain that the risk of encountering a landmine was of minimal concern when compared to continued oppression beneath the Khmer Rouge. Continued border clashes between the Khmer Rouge and Vietnam led to the eventual overtaking of Phnom Penh by Vietnamese forces, a condition seen as temporary by many Cambodians, who felt an urgency to flee the country.

More than 300,000 Cambodians lived within refugee camps on both sides of the Cambodia–Thailand border by June of 1979 (Gottesman, 2003). Dozens of camps housed basic amenities for thousands of forlorn, fleeing individuals and families from all factions, including Khmer Rouge soldiers as well as defectors. Although they detested each other, a common distaste for the occupying Vietnamese established a commonality between the groups sufficient to allow civility within camps.

In addition to travel toward international borders, many Cambodians sought food, having experienced starvation for nearly 4 years. Genocidal captors and civilian prisoners alike utilized knowledge concerning the whereabouts of food-stock warehouses and headed toward the numerous provincial capitals dotting the landscape. Food stocks were packed in baskets and barrels along with basic cooking utensils. Cambodians continued their journeys toward hometowns and country borders in all directions. In spite of the military abandonment of food-stock facilities, the multiple warehouses containing rice throughout Cambodia were guarded by silent and dormant soldiers, the landmines. Established routes of travel eventually diluted the impact landmines could have when warehouse raids occurred until new groups arrived without the benefit of knowledge the previous group had acquired.

2.3.3. Compulsory Travel

Not all travel taking place in Cambodia was voluntary. Both the Vietnamese and Thai made decisions that significantly influenced rates of travel and led to the occurrence of numerous travel-specific landmine incidents in post–Khmer Rouge Cambodia.

The first imposition of travel occurred near the Cambodia–Thailand border. In spite of the enormous international effort to ameliorate the suffering of millions following the ousting of the Khmer Rouge, limits were quickly reached in refugee camps on the Thailand side of the border. Since the Royal Thailand Army was unable to accommodate the ever-increasing population flowing into the refugee camps, a decision was made to impede further migrations from Cambodia by securing the border. In addition, the realization among those already within Thai camps that food supplies were inadequate initiated an effort to force a sizable proportion of the refugee population back across the Cambodian border.

In June of 1980, the Royal Thailand Army forced more than 45,000 Cambodian refugees across the north border point adjacent to the Preah Vihear province (Courtois, 1999). Safe passage beyond contaminated border crossings was not offered, and passage was made on foot through the thick and dangerous terrain. Any attempt at circumventing the forced repatriation process was thwarted by Thai soldiers and their intimidating display of arsenal.[20] Border camp capacity limitations were not universally known, and subsequent population flows continued to arrive at the border in search of relief. Hundreds of thousands traveled the distance to the border only to be turned away.

Forced repatriation practices continued to take place. In July of 1989, the office of the United Nations High Commissioner for Refugees (UNHCR) was given active control of repatriation by the Secretary General of the United Nations. Plans were subsequently enacted to evaluate available land, organize populations, induce the "voluntary" repatriation of Cambodians living abroad, and implement the intermittent repatriation of Cambodians living in border refugee camps.

In March of 1992, the United Nations Transitional Authority in Cambodia (UNTAC) began the repatriation of 362,200 Cambodians from border refugee camps (Brown, 1998). This process involved mass shipping of nearly 10,000 refugees weekly to six reception centers located in Mongol Borei, Battambang, Sanke, Mong Russei, Pursat, and Phnom Penh (Courtois, 1999). It took nearly 7 months to complete the refugee-repatriation process. Initial surveys of land judged virtually all untenanted land free from landmine contamination, but when repatriation commenced in March of 1992, UNTAC delivery teams found that the previous claims about contamination-free land were greatly overstated.[21]

When it was discovered that the safety of land was greatly overestimated, a revision of repatriation took place. In an effort to succeed in repatriating refugees before the fast-approaching voting deadline in May of 1993, UNHCR reconsidered the movement of people and devised various repatriation options, which were offered to Cambodian refugees as substitutes for the initial plan. Throughout April 1992, land known to be clear of landmines was used when repatriating Cambodians while contingent plans were formulated.

UNHCR had offered each family 2 hectares of agricultural land and basic materials to build a house, according to the availability of land and the outcome of the initial land survey. After UNHCR learned the limitations of the previous land surveys regarding landmine safety, refugees were offered several choices (Brown, 1998). The first option included the original 2 hectares of land and additional materials for a house with a cash stipend of $20 per family. The second option involved only cash payments amounting to $50 per adult and $25 per child younger than 12 years old. The third option provided a kit of tools specific to a nonagricultural business such as carpentry, electrical work, or bicycle repair. All three options included basic household cooking supplies and food for 1 year (6 months for those repatriating to Phnom Penh).

The first option was unattractive to most Cambodians. First, many Cambodians were unsure of where they wanted to live, being torn between a desire to live where they had before the war and a desire to live where their families were presently located.[22] Second, after learning initial surveys of land were unsatisfactory and UNHCR's land allocation would inevitably include the contaminated land within repatriation plans, many Cambodians were reluctant to choose this plan. The third option was also not enticing because the toolkits were valued at less than the monetary equivalent of the second option, and kits were often distributed randomly, without consideration for preferences or prior skills.[23]

Eventually, more than 80% of repatriating refugees opted for the second choice. Food rations were provided for repatriating families at commune- and village-level holding centers. The unwillingness of government leaders to continue shuffling around populations in addition to the immobile nature of food supply persuaded Cambodians to remain at their current residences, at least until food rations were exhausted.[24] Throughout the year preceding the elections, many Cambodians practiced farming in their new environments. More than one in three repatriating refugees between the ages of 15 and 35 had either never farmed or had done so only during the Khmer Rouge era, when agrarian efforts were often fruitless (Gottesman, 2003). Frustration with the land-apportioning process that would normally have instigated further travel was counteracted by the guarantee of food in current areas. Although effective through the voting process, Cambodians recognized that they would soon need to provide for their own subsistence. Acknowledging the eminent and approaching deadline, many began preparing to travel upon exhausting their share of food stock.

March 30, 1993, marked the closure of Site #2, the last refugee camp on the Cambodia–Thailand border (Martin, 1989). Many Cambodians who had delayed repatriation were finally forced to re-enter Cambodia. For those repatriating late in the game, fear that the most productive land had already been occupied was prevalent. Regrettably, their fears were justified. As Cambodians crossed the Cambodia–Thailand border, they found that the only land available was contaminated. Many Cambodians made the best of their new situations by attempting to sow and reap, while others continued onward in search of productive land or family that would take them in. Eventually, many Cambodians repatriating late found themselves setting up camp in provincial urban centers. None of the final camp closures offered travel accommodations, which subsequently led to a movement of forced on-foot travel.

The Vietnamese also undertook endeavors that uprooted hundreds of thousands. When Vietnamese forces invaded Cambodia in 1979, an initiative involving securing national borders quickly followed. After several invasions of their own land by the Chinese, the Vietnamese had become accustomed to practices of border sealing. Not only would a solid border prevent the Khmer Rouge from regaining military command on Cambodian soil, but the Vietnamese also had prerogatives of protecting Vietnam from Thailand-led intrusions, and doing so on the Western border of Cambodia provided an extra layer of protection. Border-sealing practices during the Vietnamese occupation of Cambodia became known by the acronym K5.

The specific plan to hermetically seal the Cambodia–Thailand border consisted of constructing

> a long fortification structure composed of a 700 km canal, doubled with a wall. In the form of a strategic arc, it followed 10 km inside the Laos border to the maritime border in Koh Kong province. It was completed in regular intervals by small forts, which were not unlike the Great Wall of China. (Bottomley, 2001)

Although the construction of the K5 differed greatly from zone to zone, success was heavily dependent upon the supply of hundreds of thousands of Cambodian laborers.[25] Official records indicate that in the 1985 season alone, 1,618,400 antipersonnel mines were laid along the K5 mine belt (Bottomley, 2001). Estimates of the total number of antipersonnel landmines used in efforts to establish the K5 mine belt throughout the "K5 Era" range from 4,000,000 to 25,000,000.[26] The enormity of landmine usage near the Cambodia–Thailand border continues to plague Cambodians more than two decades beyond the completion of the project.

In order to satisfy K5 labor demands, PRK forces offered financial incentives, mandated military service for specific age groups, and finally forcibly conscripted Cambodians (Gottesman, 2003). By the end of 1984, more than 50,000 Cambodians took part in the K5 initiative.[27] A tripling of forces was accomplished throughout the 1984 to 1985 time period, thereby reflecting more than 150,000 K5 workers by December of 1985 (Gottesman, 2003). High death rates necessitated the recruitment of more workers to ensure the progress of K5. As PRK-led conscription rates increased, thousands of Cambodian families moved their belongings to more remote areas in an attempt to avoid conscription.[28]

To avoid a second summons, thousands of Cambodians continued to cross landmine-contaminated soil into Thailand in hopes of establishing roots in a land free from compulsory enlistment (Martin, 1989). A law announced in late 1985 changed the nature of conscription from a near-random selection process to a compulsory and obligatory service period for both males and females. Five years of mandatory conscription existed for males between the ages of 18 and 30. Furthermore, men 16 to 60 and women 16 to 35 were to serve in militia or self-defense units (Martin, 1989). This decree initiated a mass mobilization of the majority of the Cambodian populace in either forced military pursuits or an effort to avoid them.

A continued effort to move Cambodians to areas deemed highly productive by PRK was simultaneously at play (Gottesman, 2003). Following territorial gains from the Khmer Rouge in the 1984 to 1985 offensives, Cambodians were instructed to make use of the newly obtained terrain, despite the land being highly ordnance laden. The practice of reclaiming PRK lands, euphemistically entitled New Economic Zones, followed a similar practice that took place in Vietnam after the United States withdrew from the war there.[29] As individuals sought to plow the soil, herd animals, and collect food amid landmine-contaminated soil, incidents ensued.

In addition to conscription efforts for the PRK army, the PRK also used peasants for building projects around the country. In some instances, construction of new roads and buildings or the repair of dams and forts occupied the time of those charged with tasks (Gottesman, 2003). Compensation for labor was meager, but in some instances it was reported as having provided sufficient rice for a family of four.

PRK decisions about which individuals to task with building projects were often made on the basis of where individuals lived and who possessed land deemed valuable. Hanoi moved hundreds of thousands of Vietnamese nationals into Cambodia to serve as "masters of the land" (Gottesman, 2003), and Cambodians who had access to valuable land resources were stationed on building projects while their possessions were appropriated to the Vietnamese nationals. In spite of strong personal connections with previous "lands of inheritance," many Cambodians made decisions to relocate away from Vietnamese-dominated zones without having a clear direction about where to move.

Some Cambodians abandoned their property in fear of it being appropriated, acknowledging that "it is better to lose land than to lose land

and be conscripted."[30] In August of 1982, the then-current mayor of Phnom Penh, Kaev Chenda, forcibly rounded up 500 families from the capital city and sent them to the Svay Rieng without even receiving permission from the Council of Ministers (Gottesman, 2003). Remaining Cambodians were threatened by this display of power. Consequent to these actions, several other Cambodian families followed the movement to Svay Rieng, while others worked harder at producing rice in an effort to avoid conscription in a second directive. The Romeas Haek, Rumduol, and Svay Teab districts within the Svay Rieng province all suffered travel-related landmine incidents at higher-than-prevalent rates during this time period.

2.3.4. Property Rights and Travel

On October 13, 1992, land and property rights were drastically altered, which subsequently increased travel throughout Cambodia. The National Assembly changed Cambodia from a centrally controlled society to a market-based economy. Under the definition of Article 19, a reinstatement of the legal principle of the Civil Code of 1920 was enacted (East-West Management Institute [EWMI], 2001). This law stated that ownership of land was considered "the right to enjoy and dispose of property according to the desires of individuals." Traditional practices of land titling, succession, possession, and contracts of sale were re-enacted. Squatter rights were recognized contingent on a 5-year possession claim, which subsequently led to the flight of Cambodians in an effort to claim land. A general fear that land reclamation rights would be halted caused an increased rate of land-claim travel to occur for years following the 1992 Land Law Act, peaking in 1996. The Royal Government of Cambodia issued a proclamation in November 1995 stating that squatter rights would be abolished in the coming months. Land cultivated before the expiration of squatter rights would be considered the legal property of the individual. Land not cultivated would become property of the state. This proclamation motivated thousands of Cambodians to travel and expand their ownership of land.

2.4. Tampering Landmine/UXO Incidents

Tampering is defined as intentional engagement with landmines/UXO with an interest of benefiting economically from the sale, transfer, or use thereof. Ordnance can include metal casings, explosives, and fuses, all of which can be sold separately within Cambodia. Fuses are sold to fisherman and explosives to miners, and metal eventually makes it to the international market. The nature of tampering in Cambodia changed drastically following the rapid industrialization of China. As China industrialized, Chinese metal exports to Thailand declined, driving up the price in Thailand. Cambodia responded to the higher price by exporting postwar scrap.

Section 2.4.1 describes tampering as an incident category. Section 2.4.2 explains the historical underpinnings of the rise of tampering in Cambodia.

2.4.1. Tampering Defined

I define tampering-related incidents as intentional interaction with ordnance by individuals or groups in an effort to benefit economically from the action. Currently, tampering is more narrowly defined by mine-action practitioners because they only consider overt admissions of "handling" as legitimate. Measuring tampering incidents by means of overt admissions of handling alone severely undercounts the economically driven incidents. Accordingly, I define tampering from the perspective of an economist with the goal of linking tampering to primary intentions to interact with ordnance. Capturing tampering in this way will enable policy makers and the mine-action community to view tampering from an incentives-based approach and accordingly target the reduction of incidents that fall into this category.

I distinguish between an accident and tampering on the basis of responses to postincident interviews with victims of or witnesses to the event. These questions attempt to identify the type of activity taking place when the incident occurred. Incidents that took place while burning (agriculturally related), clearing new land for development, collecting food, cutting/collecting, farming, herding, labor, military activity, playing (not with landmine), and traveling (for landmine-related incidents only) are categorized as accidental occurrences. Fishing, handling the mine/UXO, "nothing—exploded beside," no answer, and traveling (for UXO incidences only) are categorized as the outcome of intentional engagement with ordnance, or tampering. Defining tampering in this way more accurately reflects the economic incentives underlying ordnance-seeking behavior.

The most obvious activity in the tampering category is handling. Handling the mine/UXO is an overt admission of tampering. The proportion of respondents openly admitting handling ordnance has decreased over time because this activity became illegal and punishable by fines and jail time. Fishing incidents occur while using either the fuses from ordnance or the landmine-related ordnance to fish. Fishing incidents do not include individuals traveling with intent to fish but rather those using ordnance in fishing.

The response of "nothing—exploded beside" and no response also suggest tampering. The proportion of individuals responding in these ways prior to tampering becoming illegal comprised 0.5% of the total incidents. After tampering becoming illegal, it climbed to 9.1% of the total incident count. This suggests respondents are trying to avoid the punitive consequences associated with tampering.

Traveling incidents involving UXO are also indicative of tampering. UXO-specific incidents occur primarily in the western half of Cambodia, whereas the majority of UXO-specific ordnance lies in the eastern half of Cambodia. This implies that individuals are discovering UXO in the east and traveling to the west in order to sell the ordnance to Thailand.

2.4.2. History of Tampering

Although tampering incidents used to be small both in magnitude and as a share of total incidents, since 1996, this is no longer the case. As was shown in Figure 2.2, since 2000, tampering-related incidents are the most prevalent form of incident occurrence. The nature of landmine/UXO incidents in Cambodia has shifted away from accidental, agrarian, and travel-specific activities and now primarily involves intentional interaction with ordnance in the form of tampering.

One major factor giving rise to this drastic change is the economic expansion of China. As China embarked upon a process of rapid industrialization in the early 1990s, former practices of exporting metal to various countries were reduced in order to meet domestic needs.[31] Thailand was one of the countries experiencing a decrease in metal imports from China, causing the price of metal to rise.[32] In response to high prices for metal, Thailand's eastern neighbor, Cambodia, offered post-war scrap. The price of metal in Cambodia's western neighbor, Thailand, has remained substantially higher than that in Vietnam to the east.[33]

Consequently, UXO is often transported the entire distance of the country to the Thai border in pursuit of a higher price. As was shown in Figure 2.3, tampering-related incidents occur in the greatest magnitude near the Thai border in spite of the fact that most UXO originates from the other side of the country. The substantial increase in tampering incidents reflected throughout the post–2000 era is therefore likely to be linked to the rising price of metal.

ENDNOTES

1. Government and nongovernment organizations contributing to landmine-related data collection processes include Royal Cambodia Armed Forces (RCAF), Mines Advisory Group (MAG), Hazardous Area Life-Support Organization (HALO), Norwegian People's Aid (NPA), Compagnia Francaise d'Assistance Specialisee (COFRAS), and the United Nations Mine Clearance and Training Unit (UNMCTU).
2. Contributions to Cambodia's mine-action sector are contingent upon results with previously donated funds. Nations contributing to landmine/UXO clearance in Cambodia within the 1997 to 2006 time frame include Australia, Belgium, Canada, China, Denmark, European Union, Finland, France, Germany, Ireland, Japan, Luxembourg, the Netherlands, New Zealand, Norway, South Korea, Spain, Sweden, Switzerland, the United Kingdom, and the United States. The United Nations Development Programme (UNDP) and individual donors have also contributed financially to mine-action programs.
3. Questionnaires for landmine/UXO victims have changed and evolved over time. An example of the most recent questionnaire is provided with permission from Chhiv Lim, director of CMVIS, in Appendix C.
4. These calculations exclude military-related incidents from the observation set. If we include military incidents in the observation set, we find that landmine-related incidents range from a low of 350 in 2007 to a high of 4,674 in 1980. Military-specific landmine/UXO incidents are not the focus of this study and have therefore been left out of the core analysis.
5. Observations are pooled for the years 1980 through 2007.
6. A value greater than 0.2 indicates positive spatial autocorrelation. It is evident that positive spatial autocorrelation exists for each incident activity.
7. The existence of positive spatial autocorrelation suggests that neighboring observations affect each other.
8. Slaughter of livestock caused complications in the following agricultural seasons. Buffalo are used in the rice-preparation process, and the lack of buffalo therefore constituted a problem in agricultural production.
9. In addition, a large proportion of the rice seed stock was taken by fleeing Khmer Rouge forces. According to N.O., an ex-Khmer Rouge soldier, the majority of rice seed stock was located near the Thailand border in anticipation of Vietnamese invasion. Repeated Khmer Rouge border encroachments into Vietnam irked the Vietnamese army and caused several

small-scale battles. Both armies had interests in extending the ill-defined border, which, according to N.O., was the ultimate cause of Vietnamese occupation in Cambodia.

10. International donations made to distribution units in Thailand, although influential in alleviating suffering, were also feeding the Thai soldiers guarding the refugee camps. People's Republic of Kampuchea (PRK) forces were not subject to the same degree of starvation as Cambodians because they had preferential access to food stocks in addition to more than 10,000 tons of rice, 10,000 tons of rice seed, 9,000 tons of fuel, and large shipments of tools and equipment from Hanoi and Moscow. This information was cited by the Ministry of Agriculture in Phnom Penh, and also quoted in Gottesman (2003). Khmer Rouge soldiers were also not subject to the degree of starvation that the rest of the country endured. Western European nations and the United States were not willing to send supplies of food to the areas of Cambodia that were in the greatest need because this would require interaction with the Vietnamese occupiers.
11. When farmers in Prasat Sambour were given high-yielding rice seed to plant in the fall of 1996, a collective decision was made not to plant with the new seed stock. My research indicates that some farmers planted a portion of their fields with the new stock and found out that *if* a harvest was reaped, it was substantial. However, the risk of harvest was great, and many were not in a position to shoulder this risk. A major subsidization of high-yielding rice stock took place in 1996. Although many farmers did not plant the high-yielding varieties, enough did use these varieties in the planting process, leading to a vast increase in rice production during this time period.
12. The Tonle Sap (a combined lake/river system) is located in the center of Cambodia. This lake flows southward into the Gulf of Thailand for half of the year and then changes direction and pulls water from the Gulf into the heart of Cambodia.
13. S. H., a rice farmer in the Phnom Srok district (1984–1989), initially attempted to meet the high demands of PRK by planting rice in locations that were considered risky. The risk associated with planting in specific areas included rough terrain, less-productive soil, and potentially landmine-contaminated ground. S. H. continued this practice for two seasons until his entire seed stock was used up. Production levels were slightly greater than in previous seasons, but S. H. never received any reward for his increased productivity. Consequent to this experience, S. H. began siphoning enough rice to meet subsistence before reporting to local authorities. There is a general consensus that this phenomenon was widespread.

14. It is important to note that there may be an undercounting of landmine-related incidents occurring during this time period attributed to the loss of food. Specifically, numerous K5 workers abandoned their posts in search of food. These individuals' incidents were classified as military incidents and are therefore not captured in the civilian statistics, but they are nonetheless critically linked to issues of food supply and landmine-related incidents.
15. Rice production during the K5 Era took place under the charge of collective mandates. Theoretically, rice was collected from farmers throughout Cambodia and redistributed according to need after meeting administrative quotas. However, rice was rarely distributed. Y. S., a farmer who lost his entire crop during the 1984 to 1985 agricultural seasons, went to his provincial head to request enough food provisions to meet subsistence for himself, his wife, his mother, and his four daughters. Y. S. was informed that rice was not being redistributed in cases of drought or flood because there was simply not any rice to spare. Furthermore, Y. S. was told that if there was rice to spare, it would be prioritized to soldiers working on the K5 mine belt. The unwillingness of PRK leaders to provide rice for those who had unsuccessful harvest cycles was commonplace.
16. The leadership of PRK required quotas from province officials each rice harvest cycle. Filling quotas was not according to a systematic process. Many Cambodians were frustrated and angered about Vietnamese food appropriations. Rice extractions increased in demand and frequency led many Cambodians to support anti-Vietnamese forces (Khmer Rouge) in an effort to oust the new enemy from Cambodia.
17. From the author's conversation with C. L. and S. S., March 2003, in the Sompov Meas district. Both individuals were unaware of the status of their children in early 1979 but were informed of holding centers in Vietnam where orphans were being held. C. L. and S. S. both walked for weeks in an effort to reach the Cambodia–Vietnam border.
18. When C. L. reached a Vietnamese orphan holding center in March of 1979, he was instructed that formal documentation was required before he could enter the center to search for his children. C. L. was unable to locate any documentation at his former place of residence and later found that all of his children had died during Pol Pot's reign. S. S. reached a different holding center in Vietnam in April of 1979, where she found one of her missing daughters. S. S. was informed that a release fee was required before her daughter could be released from the center. S. S. traveled on foot for 8 days to the Chhloung district in the Kracheh province, where her sister's

residence was before the Khmer Rouge, in search of valuables to pay the release fee. S. S.'s daughter was released in 1981.

19. Spatial analysis of landmine-related incidents occurring during this time period clearly indicates that the epicenter of landmine/UXO incidents existed near the Cambodia–Vietnam border, a phenomenon that did not occur again in this magnitude until after 2000.
20. Information obtained by author through meetings with S. K. in March of 2003. S. K., a native of Thailand, was stationed on the Cambodia–Thailand border during the June 1980 repatriation across the Cambodia border. S. K. remembers a Cambodian mother and child who, after being released from the delivery truck, resisted the repatriation effort. Both the mother and child were shot by Thailand border protectionists to prevent any further opposition to the action. S. K. resigned from the Thai military the next day.
21. As evidence of the understatement of landmine/UXO incidents, traditional March incident counts are compared across the years. A staggering 12.5% of travel-specific landmine/UXO incidents occurred in the month of March in 1992 following refugee repatriation. This figure can be compared to an average of 9.4% of annual incidents that occurred during the month of March throughout the 3 years preceding and following 1992. The increase in landmine/UXO incidents can be attributed to travel-specific incidents occurring in transport regions.
22. Before repatriating, Cambodians were often not aware of the location of family members or even if family was still alive. By accepting the first option, individuals would be subjecting themselves to a designated plot of land that may or may not be close to relatives. For many, this was much too great a risk.
23. This option was also unattractive because Cambodians were unsure that the promised supplies would be delivered. Promises from the Khmer Rouge and the PRK were often not kept, and Cambodians saw no reason why they should suddenly trust the pledge of UNHCR representatives.
24. Often, families decided to relocate to a specific urban center only to find that family was not nearby. Many families sent one member of the family to other urban centers in search of relatives while the remaining family members waited at the initial station.
25. J. B., a witness of the construction of K5, described it as being "around 2 km wide, with first a 500-meter strip of clear terrain, then a fence, a mine field, another fence, and then more clear terrain."
26. Estimates of antipersonnel landmine usage rates vary considerably between official and unofficial records. Official records kept by PRK officials

indicate purchases of 4,000,000 antipersonnel mines between 1984 and 1989 to be used for purposes of "securing the border with Thailand." Although this figure reflects a recorded number of antipersonnel landmines purchased for use on the K5 mine belt, an unofficial figure as high as 26,000,000 antipersonnel landmines has also been anecdotally stated. S. S., a 48-year-old military veteran, was in charge of distributing antipersonnel landmines, firearms, and sometimes food to conscripted PRK armies during the K5 project. S. S. noted that only a fraction of antipersonnel landmines were officially recorded on PRK documents. Antipersonnel mines were often provided PRK forces in exchange for timber, rice and gems. He estimated that for every shipment of officially recognized provisions, there were seven that were received unofficially. C. R. worked on the K5 minefield project between 1986 and 1989 in the Banteay Ampil, Thma Pouk, and Svay Chek districts. During that time, he supervised mine-laying troops and transported them to and from sites. He estimates that for every military-related landmine incident that occurred, 3,000 mines were successfully planted. Accordingly, with 7,145 military-related incidents occurring during the K5 Era, 21,435,000 mines were planted.

27. Official PRK records indicate more than 50,000 K5 workers by the end of 1984 (Bottomley, 2001). Official PRK records primarily indicate conscripted Cambodians. The 50,000 figure, therefore, does not include volunteers, non-K5 conscriptions, leadership of K5 projects, or Vietnamese armies present on K5 projects.
28. In 1982, the Council of Ministers instructed local PRK authorities to forcibly recruit able-bodied men and women between the ages of 17 and 25. In many instances, families followed a conscription order, which often resulted in resettling choices involving mine-contaminated land.
29. New Economic Zone planning was a practice that Vietnam found useful after the United States withdrew. The establishment of specific zones helped reorient people into areas that were deemed appropriate by authorities. Reasons for the establishment of New Economic Zones included diminishing urban movements, taking advantage of high-productivity soil, creating new urban centers, and protecting borders by establishing new towns.
30. Quote is from C. E. in March 2003. C. E. voluntarily moved away from Vietnamese-controlled land in 1981 in order to avoid conscription.
31. By 1998, China was exporting 37% less rolled steel than it had been 3 years previously in 1995. In addition to the reduction of steel exports from China, the proportion of steel exported to Thailand was more dramatically reduced. Specifically, between the years 1993 and 1995, an average of

1.2% of Chinese steel goods were exported to Thailand. This number fell to 0.8% starting in 1996. Information obtained from the National Bureau of Statistics in China (NIS, 2007).

32. Thailand Cold Rolled Steel Sheet (TCR) is the largest producer of carbon cold-rolled steel in Thailand. Author's conversations with TCR's executive director, Sakrapan Eamegol, confirmed that a sharp reduction of metal imports from China occurred in 1996. The initial supply shock was so drastic that an excess demand for metal still exists in many parts of Thailand. TCR has taken advantage of the rising prices of metal by producing to full plant capacity.
33. Vietnam, historically, has not relied on imports of metal from China to the same degree that Thailand has. According to the National Bureau of Statistics in China, Vietnamese exports totaled 20% to 60% of those of Thailand (NIS, 2007).

Chapter 3

Socioeconomics and Landmine/UXO Incident Rates

3.1. Introduction

This chapter explores the impact of socioeconomic conditions on the frequency of landmine/UXO accidents and tampering in a cross-sectional framework. Data have been compiled from the 1998 General Census of Cambodia (RGC, 1999), the 1998 Population Census of Cambodia (NIS, 2004b), and the Cambodian Mine/UXO Victim Information System (CMVIS) database (CMVIS, 2008).

CMVIS values used in this analysis include a 5-year span surrounding the 1998 census. Specifically, 1996 through 2000 will be used to reflect the dependent variable. Independent variables included in the analysis involve various socioeconomic indicators including age dependence, single-parent dependence, formal education proportions, firewood–cooking proportions, safe drinking water proportions, K5 districts, migration, population densities, rural/urban status, and sex ratios. In an effort to control for spatial effects, spatially lagged models are used when performing regressions.

The dependent variable in this analysis specifically controls for landmine/UXO incidents within separate categories of accidents and tampering. Identifying linkages between landmine/UXO incidents and the stated socioeconomic variables will assist policy makers in formulating practical plans to preempt the occurrence of landmine/UXO incidents. Following the estimation results, policy measures targeting effective means of reducing landmine/UXO incidents are considered.

This chapter is organized as follows. Section 3.2 describes the empirical model. It provides detailed information on each independent variable and establishes theoretical justification for its inclusion in the analysis. Shortcomings of data are also addressed in this section. Section 3.3 describes the empirical model. Additionally, this section explains the basic precepts of spatial autocorrelation and the need to correct for it within the modeling process. Regression outcomes are also formally presented. Section 3.4 includes interpretative discussion of the regression results. Separate regressions are performed both adjusting missing district data to values represented by geographically close neighbors and subtracting missing districts from the observation set. Section 3.5 concludes by proposing policy recommendations based on the empirical findings.

3.2. EMPIRICAL MODEL

In order to assess the impact of socioeconomic conditions on the frequency of landmine/UXO accidents and tampering incidents, I estimate the following model for a cross section of 185 districts:

$$\begin{aligned} Y_{id} = \beta_{0i} + \beta_{1i}AD_d + \beta_{2i}SPD_d + \beta_{3i}E_d + \beta_{4i}F_d + \beta_{5i}W_d \\ \beta_{6i}K5_d + \beta_{7i}M + \beta_{8i}PD_d + \beta_{9i}R_d + \beta_{10i}SR_d + e_{id} \end{aligned} \tag{3.1}$$

where i = incident, A = accident, T = tampering, and d is the district index. Y stands for the number of incidents, accidents or tampering, AD for age-dependency index, SPD for single-parent dependency ratio, E for formal education rate, F for firewood–cooking proportion, W for safe drinking water proportion, $K5$ for the K5 dummy variable, M for migration rate, PD for population density, R for rural index, and SR for the sex ratio. The β represents the coefficient on each of the independent variables.

Landmine/UXO accidents and tampering together constitute incidents. The occurrence of an incident can result in maiming, amputation, or death. Accidents are defined as the combination of both agrarian and traveling incidents. Agrarian incidents may take place during burning, being a bystander, clearing, cutting, collecting, construction, farming, herding, labor, playing, and toileting. Traveling involves accidents occurring while traveling, excluding the UXO-related travel incidents because the latter are a likely result of tampering. Tampering incidents are distinguished from accidents because they take place following intentional handling of landmines/UXO. Accidents, tampering, and incidents are all represented as the number of incidents per population of 10,000 in each district. Next, I define each independent variable and discuss its hypothesized effect on the number of each type of incident.

3.2.1. Age Dependency

Age-dependency ratio is defined as the proportion of a district's population younger than the age of 10. A higher dependency ratio signals higher poverty and economic vulnerability. Therefore, I use age-dependency proportions as a suitable measure of poverty. Young children are not physically able to carry out agrarian tasks to the degree an older individual could in spite of the fact that they still require a considerable amount of food. When the share of young children relative to the supporting population is higher, economic vulnerabilities increase, leading to a subsequent increase in landmine/UXO incidents.

Age dependency is tied to landmine/UXO incidents by means of three channels. First, age dependency is a signal of poverty, and areas more impoverished undertake tilling in more dangerous land. Areas with greater age dependence will, therefore, experience greater degrees of landmine/UXO accidents. Next, young people often tamper with ordnance as a means of making fast cash. The immediacy of monetary remuneration makes scrapping activities attractive to young children while at the same time placing them in situations of extreme risk. Third, landmine/UXO accidents would naturally positively relate with age dependency because younger children are not able to read danger warnings and lack experience carrying out safe food-acquisition activities.

3.2.2. Single-parent Dependency

Single-parent dependency ratios are constructed by pooling individuals widowed, divorced, or separated and dividing this figure by the population at the district level. Single-parent dependency ratios are also a measure for poverty. Children raised in Cambodia by both economically active parents most often live a meager existence. When children are raised by only one parent, economic pressures to provide a livelihood often force children toward risky activities such as prostitution, farming marginal lands, and metal scrapping. Accidents are likely to increase through farming. More specifically, economic need compels single parents and children of single parents to work on contaminated land. Tampering incidents are also likely to correlate directly with higher single-parent dependency ratios because individuals subject to poverty will undertake risky activities such as ordnance tampering as a means of survival.

This hypothesis, however, is subject to an important qualification. Hundreds of nongovernmental child-focused organizations exist in urban areas, especially Phnom Penh, where landmines/UXO are cleared and therefore incidents are unlikely. Therefore, the hypothesized relationship between incidents and single-parent ratio is expected to hold in rural areas.

3.2.3. Formal Education

Formal education measures the proportion of the population (above age 8) within each district that has obtained at least 1 year of formal education. More specifically, individuals who attended at least 1 year of primary school are counted as educated.[1] I use the education ratio as a proxy for wealth. A lower rate of education indicates relative lack of access to resources, therefore reflecting relative poverty. Consequently, lower rates of education imply higher susceptibility to landmine/UXO incidents through channels discussed above in cases of age and single-parent dependency. In addition, formal education could be complementary to landmine/UXO education, which is theoretically linked to a reduction in incidents.

3.2.4. Firewood–Cooking

Households in Cambodia are classified in the 1998 General Census of Cambodia according to the type of fuel used in food-preparation processes: firewood, charcoal, kerosene, gas, and electricity. Firewood–cooking ratio is defined as the share of households using firewood as their major food-preparation energy source.

Firewood, which is acquired by foraging, is the cheapest source of energy to acquire. The proportion of households acquiring firewood as their primary food-preparation energy source is, therefore, used as a proxy for poverty. Landmine/UXO incidents, critically tied to situations of poverty, can thus be indexed to a firewood–cooking ratio.

A higher firewood–cooking ratio implies a greater extent of foraging activities. As individuals attempt to gather firewood, landmine/UXO accidents are more likely to occur. Tampering incidents are also tied to the firewood–cooking ratio because as individuals experience poverty to a greater degree, people resort to tampering activities.

3.2.5. Safe Drinking Water

Safe drinking water proportions are defined as the proportion of a district's population that can afford to purchase purified water. Water can also be piped or acquired from wells, springs, rivers, streams, or lakes.

The acquisition of safe drinking water requires financial resources. The proportion of the population with access to safe drinking water is therefore a proxy for wealth. Access to safe drinking water will decrease both landmine/UXO accidents and tampering incidents because travel in search of water will decline with established trade routes of bottled water and water being piped directly to homes. With rising and falling water levels throughout the wet and dry seasons in Cambodia, water acquisition does not always take place in the same geographic location. Uncertainty about where to acquire water leads to a search process closely tied to landmine/UXO accidents. More critically, however, areas that have access to safe drinking water are less vulnerable to the ills of poverty, and their populations do not engage in food-foraging practices as often. Tampering incidents are also expected to be lower in areas with access to safe drinking water because access to water signals higher wealth.

3.2.6. K5 Districts

As explained in previous chapters, the K5 mine belt is the largest mine belt in the world. In a Vietnamese-backed government initiative, landmines were intentionally laid near the Cambodia–Thailand border in an effort to hermetically seal it. Sixteen districts along the Cambodia–Thailand border are geographically a part of the K5 mine belt. These heavily contaminated areas are captured by the inclusion of a K5 dummy variable,[2] which identifies districts that are part of the K5 mine belt with a value of 1, leaving non-K5 districts with a value of 0. This method of measurement isolates K5 districts into a category that can be directly tested as a variable in its own right.

A strong positive relationship between K5 districts and landmine/UXO incidents is expected because accidents are likely to occur at the physical location where landmines lie. Tampering incidents are also expected to be more frequent in the K5 area because much of the scrap metal finds its way to the Thailand border, and tampering incidents can occur anytime throughout the metal acquisition and selling process.

One caveat, however, is in order. Not all districts identified as K5 districts lie entirely within the mine belt. Some districts have as little as 5% of their area within areas identified as part of the K5 mine belt. It is critical for policy makers to make note of this specification when targeting policy toward specific geographic areas. District boundaries are not synonymous with the K5 mine belt and should be considered separately when implementing policy objectives.

3.2.7. Migration

Migration as a variable measures the proportion of the immigrants into a district's boundaries between 1994 and 1998 divided by the total 1998 population. Following the ousting of the Khmer Rouge armies, many people fled Cambodia. This practice reversed throughout the 1980s and 1990s as people were either forcibly or voluntarily repatriated to Cambodia. Accordingly, throughout the period of observation, net migration flows were positive in every district throughout the country until 2004.[3]

It is important to distinguish that we are not speaking about absolute numbers of migrants within each district but rather the relative increase of the population following the inflow of migrants. As a population swells, the economy has greater difficulty absorbing new arrivals into its system. A large population increase leads to a decreased absorption capacity. Those not quickly absorbed following their migration are more vulnerable.

I anticipate a positive relationship between higher migration ratios and landmine/UXO accidents. Accidents naturally occur as marginal lands are occupied in an effort to farm and forage. It is, therefore, very likely that higher rates of landmine/UXO accidents occur in areas that experienced higher proportional increases of migrant populations.

The relationship between migration proportions and landmine/UXO tampering incidents is not as clear-cut. Tampering requires a network of scrappers, which may not exist for new arrivals. Because tampering is illegal, people must build relationships of trust before engaging in tampering activities. It is not clear, therefore, whether a sufficient period has passed that would allow tampering to be positively correlated with migration proportions.

One important caveat should be mentioned in regard to migration and landmine/UXO incidents. A few districts experiencing a vast increase in migration proportions had large absorption capacities because they were previously almost entirely vacant. Following mandatory repatriation mandates, many Cambodians were bused to vacant districts in an effort to populate these areas. Several of the areas were chosen as drop sites because of their low population. These districts experienced massive increases in population proportions, but their high absorption capacity may dilute the relationship between incidents and migration. To control for this factor, I also included the population density as an independent variable.

3.2.8. Population Density

Population density is measured as the number of people living per square kilometer of land area. Statistics concerning population densities in Cambodia are available at village, commune, district, and provincial levels. Marginal lands containing landmine-related ordnance are typically avoided when population densities are low. It is likely that as population densities increase, people are pushed toward the periphery in search of farmland that can provide a livelihood for their families. Increased pressure to find farmland should, therefore, raise the probability of victimization by landmine/UXO accidents.

It is also likely that tampering incidents are positively related to population density. As populations become increasingly dense and meeting economic needs becomes more difficult, individuals are more likely to engage in risky activities such as tampering in order to continue providing for their families.

In spite of this seemingly simplistic relationship between population densities and the occurrence of landmine/UXO incidents, two important caveats deserve attention. First, landmines and UXO are not as ubiquitous in urban centers as in rural sectors of Cambodia. This means the most heavily populated urban districts are not as likely to encounter landmine/UXO incidents. This fact may dilute the measured impact population density has on landmine/UXO incidents or may completely negate the observable impacts. In an effort to control for this reality, a rural/urban dummy variable will be included in the regression equation.

Second, it is conceivable that an endogeneity bias exists between population density and landmine/UXO incidents. It is likely that landmine/

UXO incident rates influence population densities. Consequently, the estimated impact of population density on incidents would be biased. Fortunately, evidence indicates the potential for this bias is nonexistent. CMVIS datasets track individuals who have experienced landmine/UXO incidents for years following the occurrence of an incident.[4] A comparison of traditional migration proportions to the migration activities of landmine/UXO victims and their families reveals a nearly universal trend. Families experiencing landmine-related incidents were no more likely to move residence than those not experiencing a landmine/UXO incident.[5] Endogeneity between these two variables most likely does not exist because Cambodians are most often not financially capable of moving. Endogeneity may, however, become a real phenomenon as Cambodia continues to develop.

Population data for the Pousat, Anlong Veaeng, and Trapeang Prasat districts (all along the Thailand border) are missing from the dataset because they were all considered too dangerous to enter during the time the census was conducted. I proxied the values for the missing districts by taking an average of the districts in closest geographic proximity.[6] I also ran separate regressions that exclude these three districts.

3.2.9. Rural/Urban Status

The National Institute of Statistics identifies 31 of the 185 districts as being urban.[7] In order to have a finer measure than a dummy variable, I defined the rural status variable as the proportion of the population engaged in agrarian labor. Urban areas in Cambodia contain service and industry-based sectors. Urban sectors are also more densely populated, contain internationally sponsored education and health care programs, and provide a myriad of employment alternatives to the traditional agriculture-based occupations. Urban sectors were initially the focal point of landmine-removal efforts and have subsequently experienced a greater degree of clearance.

Both landmine/UXO accidents and tampering are more likely to occur in rural districts. Landmine/UXO accidents are primarily a function of using marginal and ordnance-contaminated land. Urban sectors do not focus primarily on the production of agricultural commodities, making the marginal land utilization phenomenon nonexistent. Tampering activities, which have been described as a function of vulnerability, do not take place as frequently in urban centers because vulnerability is not as severe in these sectors. Internationally sponsored aid organizations establish themselves primarily in urban centers, largely because these areas have higher population densities.

3.2.10. Sex Ratio

Sex ratio is calculated as the proportion of males to females within each district. During the time the General Census of Cambodia was performed in 1998, garment factories employed hundreds of thousands of females in urban centers. Females often make the journey to urban centers during dry seasons in an effort to contribute to individual and family resources. As females seasonally engage in industrial labor, male/female sex ratios in rural sectors shift. The lower number of active agricultural workers raises economic demand within the agricultural sector, leading to an increase in vulnerability. As a natural consequence to increased vulnerability, landmine/UXO incidents follow.

In the relative absence of women, males engage in food-foraging activities, which are traditionally a female activity. Men often believe they are free from the risks of foraging in contaminated fields and are more likely to forage for food beyond "danger" plaques. Because women are absent, men are also more likely to engage in activities not centralized around the home. Men often engage in additional travel activities to visit relatives, to visit mistresses, or in an effort to claim additional land. These activities are much more pervasive in the absence of their wives. As travel increases, landmine/UXO accidents follow. Tampering is also much more likely to occur when male/female ratios reflect greater proportions of men. Men are more likely to work in groups composed of other men when their wives are absent from the picture, where, pride often motivates them to take on high-risk, high-reward activities.

3.2.11. Collinearity Matrix of Independent Variables

The collinearity matrix of independent variables is presented in Table 3.1. As can be seen in this matrix table, several strong relationships exist between independent variables. Single-parent dependency ratio is strongly negatively correlated with sex ratio. This relationship appropriately indicates that single-parent dependency is typified by female-headed households. Firewood–cooking ratio is strongly positively correlated to rural status. Not surprisingly, in more agriculture-based districts, firewood is more likely to be the primary source of cooking fuel. Finally, there is also a strong negative correlation between firewood–cooking ratio and access to safe drinking water. Again, this result is not surprising based on previous arguments.

3.2.12. Summary Statistics

Table 3.2 summarizes median values, standard deviations, and minimum and maximum values for all variables. Additionally, the anticipated relationships between each of the independent variables and landmine/UXO accidents and tampering are included in the table.

3.3. Empirical Model

In testing the relationship between landmine/UXO incidents and socioeconomic factors, I correct for spatial clustering. In cases where independent variables exhibit spatial dependence, ordinary least squares (OLS) estimation techniques are not appropriate because they lead to inefficient and biased estimates.

Tobler's First Law of Geography states "Everything is related to everything else, but near things are more related than distant things" (Tobler, 1970, p. 269). Spatial dependence exists when the value of a variable in one location is affected by the values of the variable in neighboring areas, which may be the outcome of spatial interactions, diffusion, and spillover effects. This dependence can exist in both the observed independent variables and in the error term.

TABLE 3.1. Collinearity Matrix Between Independent Variables.

	AD	SPD	E	F	W	K5	M	PD	R	SR
Age Dependency (AD)	1									
Single-Parent Dependency (SPD)	-0.25	1								
Education (E)	**-0.66**	0.34	1							
Firewood (F)	**0.59**	0.3	-0.34	1						
Water (W)	**-0.57**	-0.02	**0.39**	**-0.5**	1					
K5	0.14	**-0.42**	-0.14	-0.2	-0.06	1				
Migration (M)	-0.28	-0.34	0.08	**-0.6**	**0.44**	0.31	1			
Population Density (PD)	**-0.6**	0.1	0.31	**-0.62**	0.24	-0.05	0.25	1		
Rural (R)	**0.66**	0.18	**-0.45**	**0.76**	**-0.73**	-0.07	**-0.66**	**-0.45**	1	
Sex Ratio (SR)	0.22	**-0.72**	-0.31	-0.29	0.06	**0.47**	**0.49**	-0.1	-0.25	1

TABLE 3.2. Independent Variable Summary Statistics.*

	Statistics				Anticipated Correlation	
VARIABLE	Median	Std. Dev.	Min	Max	Landmine/UXO Accidents	Landmine/UXO Tampering
Accidents	0.77	24.91	0	161		
Tampering	0.96	5.92	0	37.33		
Incidents	2.18	30.19	0	189.8		
Age-Dep.	0.29	0.03	0.2	0.35	Increase	Increase
Single-Parent Dep.	0.05	0.01	0	0.08	Increase	Increase
Education	0.52	0.15	0	0.83	Decrease	Decrease
Firewood	0.97	0.16	0.1	1	Increase	Increase
Water	0.01	0.13	0	0.69	Decrease	Decrease
K5 Dummy	0	0.29	0	1	Increase	Increase
Migration	0.07	0.11	0	0.73	Increase	Ambiguous
Pop. Density	98	3996	0.8	43905	Increase	Increase
Rural Index	0.85	0.25	0	1	Increase	Increase
Sex-Ratio	0.95	0.08	0.5	1.44	Increase	Increase

Note. *Dataset includes 185 Observations.

Spatial autocorrelation refers to the degree in which spatial features, along with their associated data values, exhibit patterns of clustering in space. Spatial dependence may be the outcome of the dependent variable in one location being affected by the independent variables in the neighboring locations, in which case the OLS estimates are biased and inefficient. It is also possible that spatial relationships exist outside of the measured variables and are reflected in the error term. Spatial error suggests the presence of spatially correlated omitted variables, still suggesting OLS will produce inefficient estimations. When neighboring units of observation are similar, positive spatial autocorrelation exists. When spatial dependence exists within the error term, it is appropriate to use spatial-error models. In order to verify the presence of positive spatial autocorrelation and the specificity of the type of spatial dependence, I perform both tests. Moran's I is a common measure of spatial autocorrelation.[8]

It is defined as: $I = \frac{N}{\Sigma_i \Sigma_j W_{ij}} \frac{\Sigma_i \Sigma_j W_{ij}(X_i - \overline{X})(X_j - \overline{X})}{\Sigma_i (X_i - \overline{X})^2}$, where N is the number of spatial units indexed by i and j; X is the variable of interest; $\overline{X}$ is the mean of X; and w_{ij} is a matrix of spatial weights obtained from a contiguity matrix that accounts for neighborhood pattern. Values of Moran's I greater than .2 or less than –.2 (bounded by extremes between –1 and 1) indicate positive and negative spatial autocorrelation, respectively (at the 5% significance level).

This analysis uses a queen contiguity matrix in conjunction with Moran's I in order to include every adjacent district in the observation set.[9] Tests to determine whether spatial dependence exists within the error term simply apply Moran's I calculations to OLS estimations of the error term. Moran's I tests for spatially lagged and spatial-error models confirm the presence of positive spatial autocorrelation among the independent variables used in this analysis. Positive spatial autocorrelation exists among all independent variables except population density. Tests for spatial autocorrelation in the error term prove statistically insignificant. Therefore, in an effort to avoid downward-biased inefficient parameter estimates and standard error estimates, ordinary least square regressions are replaced with controlled spatially lagged regression models. Spatial dependence test results can be observed in Table 3.3.

3.4. Estimation

Table 3.4 presents the estimation results for pooled incidents separately for both accidents and tampering. Overall, the explanatory power of each regression is quite high. There is also a substantial difference between the explanatory power these variables have specifically on accidents and tampering.

TABLE 3.3. Spatial Autocorrelation Among Independent Variables.

	Spatial-Lag		Spatial-Error	
VARIABLE*	Moran's I	Distance From Threshold	Moran's I	Distance From Threshold
Age-Dep.	0.347	0.147	0.12	-0.08
Single-Parent Dep.	0.516	0.316	0.15	-0.05
Education	0.458	0.258	0.116	-0.08
Firewood	0.276	0.076	0.193	-0.01
Water	0.342	0.142	0.157	-0.04
K5 Dummy	0.553	0.353	0.028	-0.17
Migration	0.318	0.118	0.198	0
Pop. Density	0.078	-0.122	0.167	-0.03
Rural Index	0.236	0.036	0.176	-0.02
Sex-Ratio	0.494	0.294	0.117	-0.08

Note. *Dataset includes 185 observations. Moran's I threshold is obtained at 2.

It should be borne in mind that the regressions are run not over a sample of the population but rather the entire population disaggregated into districts. It follows, therefore, that the reported levels of significance should be interpreted with care. Specifically, the standard interpretation of, say, 5% significance does not imply that by drawing more observations, the coefficient being equal to 0 would be rejected in only 5% of the samples. Significance levels are more accurately a heuristic measure of the strength of the relationship between the explanatory variable and the dependent variable.

TABLE 3.4. Regression of Socioeconomic Indicators on Landmine/UXO Incidents, Accidents and Tampering.

	Incidents	Accidents	Tampering
Age Dependency	79.62	69.71	17.37
	90.3	75.93	19.76
Single-Parent Dependency	489.47	409.06	85.26
	213.35**	179.66**	46.63**
Formal Education	–15.51	–11.85	–3.8
	12.47	10.47	2.76*
Firewood	4.44	-0.36	5.16
	16.33	13.75	3.58*
Water Access	–7.46	–5.89	–2.39
	16.23	13.66	3.55
K5	24.07	22.06	3.82
	6.08***	5.17***	1.29***
Migration	30.56	30.81	0.4
	18.17**	15.31**	3.97
Population Density	0.00034	0.0002	0.00016
	0.0005	0.00042	0.00010*
Rural	0.57	2.42	–2.49
	12.24	10.27	2.7
Sex Ratio	54.94	37.06	19.81
	26.03**	21.92**	5.69***
Constant	–98.04	–73.55	–28.21
	43.09	36.29	9.39
Lagged Dependent Variable	0.66	0.63	0.58
	0.07	0.07	0.08
R-squared	0.651	0.636	0.565
S.E of Regression	17.8	14.98	3.89

Note. Number of Observations = 185. Standard errors in parentheses. *Significant at the 10 percent level, **Significant at the 5 percent level, ***Significant at the 1 percent level.

Single-parent dependency ratio has positive coefficients for landmine/UXO accidents and tampering incidents. This variable is statistically significant at the 5% level for both accidents and tampering incidents.

The sign and statistical significance of this variable suggest that targeting the reduction of the variable can have desirable impacts on landmine/UXO accidents and tampering incidents. The magnitude of the coefficient on landmine/UXO accidents is much greater than on tampering incidents. This finding is critical for policy makers to consider when targeting the reduction of accidents.

The coefficient of the formal education variable, as anticipated, is negative but statistically significant only for tampering incidents (at the 10% level). It should be noted that whenever formal education proportions reach levels of 65% or greater, landmine/UXO accident rates are close to zero. This follows from the fact that formal education proportions are higher in urban centers, where landmines are not as prevalent.

The proportion of a district's population using firewood as its major cooking energy source is positively correlated with landmine/UXO tampering incidents. It is statistically significant at only the 10% level in tampering incidents. Surprisingly, it does not have a statistically significant impact on landmine/UXO accidents.

K5 districts are positively correlated with both landmine/UXO accidents and tampering incidents at the 1% level of significance. While this result is not surprising, it should be noted that the magnitude of the coefficient is much larger on accidents than it is on tampering. This is an important observation because many of the landmine-related organizations operating in Cambodia focus the majority of their efforts within K5 regions. This targeting strategy is much more applicable in an accident framework whereas the majority of incidents occurring in post-2000 Cambodia are now tampering specific.

Migration proportions are positively correlated with both landmine/UXO accidents and tampering incidents. Although they have a direct effect on both types of incidents, they are only significant in the case of accidents (at the 5% level). These results are in line with the hypothesized relationships. It is important to note, however, that the aggregation of landmine/UXO accidents and tampering into a single measure reflecting overall incidents is statistically insignificant.

Population density is a statistically significant determinant of tampering incidents. As population densities increase, tampering incidents increase. However, they do not have a statistically significant impact on accidents. Importantly, therefore, indicators simply tracking landmine/UXO incidents would not see the relevant relationship that exists within the specified incident category. When constructing policy aimed at reducing the landmine/UXO tampering rate, policy makers should be aware that tampering is positively correlated with population densities.

Sex ratio is statistically significant in determining both landmine/UXO accidents and tampering incidents. As hypothesized, an increased male/female ratio leads to a greater degree of vulnerability and, consequently, more landmine/UXO incidents. This finding is statistically significant at the 5% level for landmine/UXO accidents and at the 1% level for tampering. While the statistical significance is greater for tampering incidents, the coefficient on accidents is larger in absolute terms. This finding should present policy makers with a key indicator of both landmine/UXO accidents and tampering incidents.

The coefficient of age dependency on landmine/UXO accidents and tampering incidents is positive, as was expected. The coefficient in the accident equation is nearly three times larger than in the tampering equation. However, both have low levels of statistical significance. When age dependencies are plotted against landmine/UXO incidents, one sees that landmine/UXO incidents become more pervasive once 28% of the district population lies below the age of 10. Below this threshold, districts experience a great deal of variance with regard to landmine/UXO incident rates. Policy makers should therefore be aware of this relationship in spite of the large degree of variance preventing statistically significant results within the aggregated regression analysis.

Although measures of access to safe drinking water, proxied by the proportion of a district's population purchasing purified water, are negatively correlated with landmine/UXO accidents and tampering incidents, this relationship is not statistically significant. The data, however, still reveal useful information. Policy makers should make note of the critical threshold that occurs when access to safe drinking water reaches 22%. Landmine/UXO incidents dramatically drop to levels below 10 per 10,000 beyond this threshold. Policy makers should, therefore, be aware that when a greater portion of the population is able to afford purified water, landmine/UXO incident rates decline.

Rural status did not prove statistically significant for either landmine/UXO accidents or tampering incidents. Furthermore, accident rates are positively correlated and tampering rates are negatively correlated with rural status. Policy makers should note that the highest landmine/UXO accident and tampering incident rates occur in areas with a rural index greater than 50%. Although a great deal of variance exists beyond this point, a critical threshold value exists here. In light of this fact, policy makers should focus their attention on areas that are more than 50% agrarian.

3.5. Landmine/UXO Policy Enactment

This section discusses current landmine/UXO policy procedures in play in Cambodia and the ways in which information obtained in this study can more effectively benefit the landmine/UXO situation in Cambodia by means of policy enactment. Cambodia currently recognizes five pillars of landmine/UXO action. Each of these pillars has firmly established goals and requires a proportion of contract funding dollars in an effort to reach these goals. Existing pillars are listed as follows:

1. Landmine/UXO clearance and the marking of contaminated areas.
2. Mine-risk education. Efforts to educate people about the risks of landmine/UXO and encourage them to avoid tampering with ordnance.
3. Victim assistance. Medical assistance and rehabilitation services to landmine/UXO victims. Workshops are often provided, assisting amputees to gain specific skills that can be used to acquire employment.

4. Stockpile destruction. International agreements require the destruction of landmine/UXO stockpiles.
5. Advocacy. Formal actions are taken to encourage countries to participate in international treaties and conventions specifically designed to end the production, trade, and use of antipersonnel mines. Additionally, advocacy seeks to gain equal rights for individuals with disabilities caused by landmine-related ordnance.

These pillars have been created and targeted at the ordnance issue in conjunction with historical observations and bold agendas. In spite of noteworthy intentions inherent within the pillars, the changing nature of the ordnance problem in Cambodia suggests pillars should be revisited and revised. As I have pointed out, tampering incidents (primarily UXO) comprise the bulk of incidents now occurring in Cambodia. Mine-clearance practices and agendas, while valuable in reducing accidents and making land available for cultivation, will not prove successful in reducing tampering incidents. In fact, the enormity of the residual-ordnance problem in Cambodia, paired with current clearance rates, suggests many decades of continued clearance before the country becomes landmine free. A primary focus on clearing landmines from the fields ignores the real nature and magnitude of the ordnance problem in this country.

While clearance will most likely remain a critical pillar and component of mine action, an immediate shift of focus is necessary in preventing people from encountering the hazards of ordnance interaction until the country becomes mine free. The effort to reduce the human costs should target relevant measures of poverty and socioeconomics that are proven as indicators of tampering behavior. Accordingly, I suggest establishing a sixth pillar of mine action titled "accident and tampering prevention." By tracking changes in single-parent dependency, formal education, firewood–cooking proportions, migration, population densities, and sex ratios, policy makers can effectively reduce or prevent rates of accidents and tampering.

Several of the variables tested in this chapter prove successful in predicting landmine/UXO accidents and tampering. Policy makers should keep track of these variables, noting that they can change dramatically with time. Specifically, the Kaoh Soutin district in the Kampong Cham province experienced a rapid increase in single-parent proportions from 6.8% in 1998 to 9.4% in 2004 because of a substantial number of malaria-related deaths. The Smach Mean Chey district in the Kaoh Kong province has a single-parent dependency proportion that fluctuates between 2.1% and 14.8% each year according to seasonal demands of export-processing zones located in Phnom Penh. Additionally, the Srei Snam district in the Siem Reap province continually suffers from a higher single-parent proportion than the other districts in the province due to the concentration of tourism in this region. As single-parent proportions increase, landmine/UXO accidents and tampering rates also increase.

District-level administrators can actively track changes in each of these critical variables and report these changes to a central authority capable of redistributing resources. This practice will assist the mine action agencies in revamping policy to accommodate changes in various poverty and socioeconomics measures. Policy makers should also ultimately target the reduction of landmine/UXO incidents by decreasing situations of poverty and vulnerability. Poverty reduction in an effort to reduce ordnance incidents is, by itself, beyond the scope and feasibility of mine action. It is possible, however, to work with poverty-reduction initiatives by sharing information about the influence of poverty reduction within the mine-action sector and advocating for poverty reduction in accordance with mine-action objectives.

Results relating to single-parent households indicate that providing assistance to families in areas where single-parent dependency proportions are high will indirectly reduce landmine/UXO incidents. As single-parent dependency proportions decrease, landmine/UXO accidents and tampering incidents both fall, in absolute terms, more so than any other variable included in this analysis. More precisely, a 1% reduction in single-parent dependency proportions will likely reduce accidents by 409 per 10,000 and tampering by 85 per 10,000. The cost of providing aid for these individuals is low. Funding for mine action can target single-parent families and provide education assistance or direct food-purchasing subsidies. Redirecting funding from the mine-action pillar involving landmine/UXO clearance for this purpose would delay complete clearance until late in this century but would prevent those living now from encountering incidents.

Policy makers can target formal education directly by reallocating funds traditionally spent on mine-risk education toward a formal education program. In spite of the controversy about the effectiveness of mine-risk education, more than 98% of Cambodians have received training on avoiding interaction with landmine-related ordnance. Funding for this cause should therefore be redirected toward formal education—providing people with skills and training that will give them access to employment options that do not include tampering with landmines and unexploded ordnance.

Targeting the proportion of a district's population using firewood as a primary source of energy with which to cook would be useless in and of itself. This variable stands as a proxy for poverty, subsequently stating that as poverty declines, landmine/UXO tampering incidents will also decline. Policy makers should use this study, which provides evidence that tampering is a function of poverty, in an effort to reduce landmine/UXO incidents. The reduction of poverty within the mine-action community, however, is a task of monumental proportion, coming at a cost many times larger than any conceivable mine-action budget could handle.

Next, policy makers should be aware of the relationship between migration and landmine/UXO accident rates. Anything causing a considerable population movement, such as land law or property rights alterations, should be recognized as influential concerning landmine/UXO accident rates. Accordingly, government should curb dramatic population movements to prevent accidents from occurring. The relationship between these variables must be established within operating ministries in Cambodia, and migration protocol should adopt practices that incorporate accident-minimization strategies.

Population density is a variable that is difficult to alter except at great social cost. Tracking population density calculations can, however, prove valuable in predicting landmine/UXO tampering incidents and should therefore be monitored by policy makers. As an area becomes more densely populated, people are pushed toward the margin and, therefore, are more likely to engage in tampering behavior.

A 1% change in sex ratios, compared with equivalent changes in the other variables, proves to be the second most influential factor in reducing both accident and tampering rates. Policy makers would be hard-pressed to enact sex-ratio restrictions. It is possible, however, to create jobs for males in areas in which females are relocated for seasonal labor. Export-processing zones in Cambodia currently target the production of garments, specifically impacting the labor supply of women. Perhaps male-dominated manufacturing plants can coexist in regions currently housing garment factories. The cost of such an approach may actually be zero if adopting such a practice proves to be financially beneficial for all parties involved.

This analysis has established various statistically significant relationships between accidents and tampering with multiple independent variables measuring poverty and socioeconomic factors. These relationships will assist policy makers and mine-action practitioners alike not only in validating the linkages between poverty, socioeconomic factors, and landmine/UXO incidents but also in understanding the relative influence of each variable. While each statistically significant variable has been considered independently, three components of this analysis deserve additional underscoring.

First, while accidents and tampering are correlated to variables capturing single-parent dependency, K5 districts, and sex ratios, the magnitude of influence each of these variables has is much higher on accidents than on tampering. Accidents can also be predicted by using migration proportions. Accidents have historically comprised the majority of incidents occurring in Cambodia and have, therefore, been the focus of mine-action efforts. For this reason, the continuance of efforts to reduce landmine/UXO accidents by mine action practitioners should make an effort to integrate these measures in predicting future accident rates. While current approaches in mine action target the reduction of accidents geographically in the K5 districts, it is likely that accidents could more effectively be reduced by also paying attention to single-parent dependency, migration, and sex ratios.

Second, mine-action practitioners should focus a larger portion of landmine/UXO incident-reduction efforts on tampering-specific incidents. Paramount to addressing the ordnance problem in Cambodia is a focus on the largest proportion of landmine/UXO incidents: the tampering-specific ones. While accidents are primarily related to landmine-specific ordnance, the majority of tampering incidents involve interaction with UXO. The geographic concentrations of landmines exist in specific epicenters near the Cambodia–Thailand border. UXO is ubiquitously distributed throughout the country and becomes mobile as scrappers discover and attempt to sell its components. This reality has complicated attempts to reduce tampering. Several variables tested here have proven to be statistically correlated with tampering to a significant degree. Specifically, tampering is positively correlated with single-parent dependency, firewood–cooking proportions, K5 districts, population density, and sex ratios. In addition to these positive correlations, tampering is also negatively correlated with formal education. These variables can now be used by mine-action practitioners in promoting policy that will assist in reducing tampering incidents.

Finally, it is also important to note that the alpha parameter, or base value, for accidents and tampering is quite distinct. More specifically, the alpha for accidents is –73.55, whereas tampering has an alpha of –28.21. Accordingly, a less dramatic flux of variables would constitute a positive tampering reality.

Endnotes

1. This is measured by the 1998 Census according to a category labeled "never attended school" and is controlled for individuals under the age of 8.
2. These are Ou Chrov, Thma Puok, Svay Chek, Malai, Sangkae and Samlout, Sampov Lun, Phnom Proek, Kamrieng, Choam Khsant, Veal Veaeng, Anlong Veaeng, Banteay Ampil, Samraong Tong, Trapeang Prasat, Pailin, and Sala Krau.
3. This is confirmed in the Cambodian Socioeconomic Survey of 1999 and 2004 (NIS, Cambodia, 2004) and the General Census of Cambodia performed in 1998 (NIS, Cambodia, 1999).
4. CMVIS tracks victim hospitalizations, amputations, and replacement of prosthetic limbs in an effort to track progress. Accordingly, records are kept concerning addresses for victims and their families.
5. The 2004 Cambodian Socioeconomic Survey indicates that an average rate of 4.2% of families already living in Cambodia moved residence each year. This number was the same for landmine/UXO incident victims and their families.
6. The Veal Veang district in the Pousat province is geographically closest to the Smach Mean Chey district in the Koh Kong province, the Thma Bang district in the Koh Kong province, and the Phnum Kravanh district in the Pousat province. Both the Anlong Veang and Trapeang Prasat districts within the Otd'ar Mean Chey province are geographically closest to the Samrong district in the Otdar Mean Chey province, the Chong Kal district in the Otdar Mean Chey province, the Varin district in the Siem Reap province, the Choam Khsant district in the Preah Vihear province, and the Kuleaen district in the Preah Vihear province.
7. These districts are Serei Saophoan, Svay Pao (Thmar Koul), Kampong Cham, Kampong Chhnang, Chbar Mon, Stueng Saen, Kampong Bay, Ta Khmau, Smach Mean Chey, Kracheh, Saen Monourom, Chamkar Mon, Doun Penh, Prampir Meankkakra, Toul Kouk, Tbaeng Mean Chey, Kampong Leav, Sampov Meas, Ban Lung, Siem Reap, Mittakpheap, Prey Nob, Stueng Hav, Stueng Traeng, Svay Rieng, Doun Kaev, Samraong Tong, Damnak Chang'aeur, Kaeb, Pailin, and Sala Krau.
8. Typical indices of spatial autocorrelation include Moran's I, Geary's C, Ripley's K, and joint count analysis.
9. A queen contiguity matrix considers each surrounding geographic unit of observation as relevant. Other possibilities include rook, bishop, and higher-order contiguity matrices.

Chapter 4

Agriculture and Landmine/UXO Incidents

4.1. Introduction

More than 70% of Cambodia's workforce operates in the agrarian sector.[1] Rice farming is the principal agricultural activity. Rice also comprises, on average, nearly 83% of the caloric intake for Cambodians (Meas, personal communication, May 7, 2008).[2] Despite the focus on the production of rice in Cambodia, net rice production levels are highly volatile across space and time. They vary with factors such as the availability of water, the varieties of rice planted, crop diversification, and natural disasters (droughts, floods, and insect infestation). When rice harvests fail and people are unable to substitute rice with other food, their situation of desperation is likely to increase. Decisions made in times of desperation often place individuals at considerable risk for landmine/UXO incidents, which likely lead to increased rates of incident occurrence.

This chapter hypothesizes that adverse agricultural conditions raise landmine-/UXO-related accidents and tampering incident rates. This hypothesis is statistically investigated and important discoveries are unveiled. When individuals suffer a rice shortage, they begin to forage for food, often in marginal lands contaminated with landmines/UXO.[3] They also often make decisions to safeguard against additional rice shortages in future periods by tilling and preparing marginal lands for cultivation. Children are also involved in the effort to mitigate the impact of a rice shortage and frequently travel into contaminated fields to scrounge for wild berries, roots, and tubers. As these activities commence, landmine/UXO accidents follow.

Landmine/UXO tampering episodes also increase when individuals become susceptible to agricultural vulnerability. People intentionally seek ordnance metal in an effort to compensate for the shortage of food, leading to increased rates of tampering incidents.

In this chapter, I statistically explore the relationships between various measures of agricultural conditions and landmine/UXO incidents. This relationship will be examined separately for both accidents and tampering. The unit of observation throughout this chapter is the province, because there are no observations on the agricultural conditions at a more disaggregated level. Although there are only 26 provinces used in this analysis, observations are available for the 1998 through 2006 period, which permits the use of panel analysis, helping to control for unobserved province-level attributes in the form of fixed effects. Incidents, accidents, and tampering, all serving as unique dependent variables, are measured relative to provincial population (per 10,000).

Section 4.2 introduces the agricultural variables and discusses their anticipated effects on both accident and tampering rates. This section also specifies variable origins, proxy estimations, and limitations of each measure of agricultural vulnerability included as a part of the econometric model. Additionally, this section formalizes the empirical model tested. Section 4.3 presents regression results. Section 4.4 proposes policy recommendations and concludes.

4.2. Agricultural Vulnerability

The staple crop in Cambodia is rice. The production level of rice depends on the availability of water, rice varieties used, land allocated to rice, and natural disasters that occur in the form of droughts, floods, and insect infestation. In addition, agricultural needs are also affected by the ability to substitute rice with other crops in times of production shortages.

The output of rice per capita reflects the overall picture of the availability of rice at the provincial level. The overall relationship between rice output and landmine/UXO accidents, however, is ambiguous. Two conflicting factors confound the net effect of rice per capita on accidents. The first effect is that higher quantities of rice reduce the incentives to seek agricultural alternatives. When rice is abundant, additional foraging practices are not necessary, which subsequently decreases the likelihood of a landmine/UXO accident occurring.

The second effect follows from the fact that a greater quantity of rice may be the result of cultivating marginal lands—a condition that would lead to an increased prevalence of accidents. Theoretical justification, therefore, exists linking net rice per capita to accidents with both a negative and positive correlation. The net effect of this divergence is unclear.

In contrast to the ambiguous nature between per-capita rice production and landmine/UXO accidents, rice production is most likely correlated with tampering in a negative direction. Tampering activities take place out of necessity. As rice becomes more abundantly available, agricultural vulnerability decreases, which is most likely to reduce the need to engage in tampering activities.

Rice yield information was originally obtained in gross yield tonnage annually for each province between 1999 and 2006. This figure was adjusted to net quantity in an effort to measure agricultural vulnerability more accurately by subtracting reseeding requirements, milling process losses, and postharvest losses. The net quantity is then expressed in per-capita terms. Average net rice per capita was 0.168 tons over the period, although there were substantial variations across space and time.

It is critical to understand the process of adjustment from gross to net values of rice. The first adjustment made allowance for seed stock and postharvest losses. The Ministry of Agriculture estimates that 13% of the gross rice yield is used in reseeding or lost in transit.[4] In obtaining reseeding values, gross figures have been adjusted to include the acreage lost to natural disasters before subtracting 13% from the inventory. Importantly, therefore, in order to obtain an accurate estimation of reseeding requirements, acreage lost to natural disaster has been included in the analysis.

Of the crop remaining after adjusting for reseeding requirements, only 64% has historically been converted into milled rice for human consumption.[5] The sizeable amount lost in the milling process, although appearing as a direct loss in regard to human consumption, provides an enormous amount of calories to large livestock. Following the general agreement of Ministry of Agriculture authorities regarding the magnitude of loss occurring during the milling process, values have been reduced by 36% in an effort to reflect this fact.

After obtaining net rice values following this process, this value is then compared to the population of each specific province during that specific year. Provincial-level population estimates were compiled by the Center for Population Studies at the Royal University of Phnom Penh in June of 2004 (NIS, 2004b). Early population reports from the 2008 General Population Census of Cambodia indicate accurate estimations in the prior report.

The relationship between net rice production and landmine/UXO incidents may be weaker in urban areas such as Phnom Penh. Net rice production per capita is quite low in Cambodia's most urbanized center, but landmine/UXO accidents and tampering incidents are very close to zero. This factor, which contradicts the hypothesized relationship, will be controlled for.

4.2.1. Supply of Water

Production of rice is almost entirely contingent on the supply of water. Rice cultivation can receive water from three major sources in Cambodia: irrigation channels, the overflow from the Tonle Sap, and rainwater. Irrigation channels reduce the risk of flooding and provide a sufficient amount of water to typically arid areas. This method of growing rice is superior to the other two because it limits agricultural vulnerability by directly controlling the level of water in rice fields. Ancient Angkorian kings understood this principle when they commenced countrywide construction projects to establish a massive network of irrigation ducts across Cambodia's landscape.

The best alternative to irrigation comes from the overflow of water near the Tonle Sap starting in mid-May and continuing until late October each year. As the Tonle Sap overflows from a dry-season volume of 3,000 square kilometers to a rainy-season volume exceeding 10,000 square kilometers, thousands of rice fields concentrically surrounding this waterway directly benefit (Figure 4.1). While the overflow of this massive waterway can be regular, the degree of flooding is highly unpredictable, leading to a degree of agricultural vulnerability not experienced in areas with irrigation control.

Farmers plant rice in anticipation that water will reach their fields at specific times and to a degree that will facilitate the growth of their crops. If water does not reach their fields, comes too early or late, or arrives in volumes too shallow or deep for the specific planted varieties, crops fail to grow. Hence, relying exclusively on Tonle Sap flood plains is riskier than irrigation flooding.

While rainwater is undoubtedly the least reliable source of water, it is the only source for the majority of Cambodian farmers. After the destruction of the majority of irrigation channels by the Khmer Rouge, today, only 20% of Cambodia's rice fields are fed by irrigation, leaving the vast majority of rice fields to the whims of nature (Meas, personal communication, May 7, 2008).[6]

The presence of irrigation channels is a prerequisite to dry-season farming. As the proportion of dry- to wet-season farming increases,

FIGURE 4.1. Traditional Floodplain Regions Throughout Cambodia.

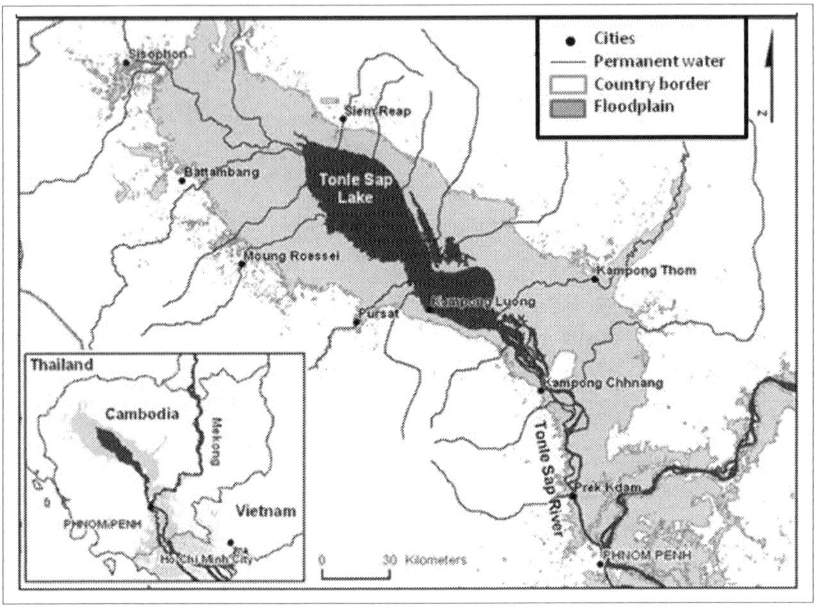

it is likely that landmine/UXO accidents and tampering incidents will decline. While both accidents and tampering share a negative correlation with dry- to wet-season rice ratios, specific theoretical underpinnings show how they are related. In regard to landmine-related accidents, a greater proportion of dry- to wet-season crop growth indicates greater utilization rates of highly productive land. On the contrary, when the vast majority of crops are grown in wet seasons, it becomes necessary to plant crops in marginal lands more likely to be contaminated with landmine-related ordnance. When these marginal lands become a part of agricultural planting choices, landmine-related accidents are more likely to occur. Higher dry- to wet-season ratios are, therefore, likely to lead to decreased rates of landmine/UXO accidents.

Landmine/UXO tampering incidents are more likely to occur in areas having low proportions of dry-season cultivation for two reasons.

First, as the vast majority of rice is available only in the wet season, vulnerabilities increase during the dry season, leading to tampering-related behavior. Second, when there is less dry-season farming, the landscape becomes arid and makes tampering activities a more practical activity. Searching for metal scrap in marshy and swampy conditions is nearly impossible given the current search methods used in Cambodia, which involve metal-detection devices. The combination of increased vulnerabilities and more convenient tampering conditions, which are both related to low dry- to wet-season ratios, creates an environment in which landmine/UXO tampering incidents are more likely to abound.

The supply of water is proxied by the hectares of rice cultivated in the dry season relative to the wet season. Cultivating land for rice production takes place year-round in areas with sufficient supplies of water. Limitations of water are reflected in the proportion of hectares planted during the wet season and not planted during the dry season. Agricultural vulnerability has been linked to the supply of water. No data exist regarding a more specific and preferable provincial measure of access to irrigation.

4.2.2. Rice Varieties

Numerous varieties of rice are planted year-round in Cambodia, with varying degrees of productivity. Cambodia is continually pressured by the international community to adopt higher-yield rice varieties. While the potential yield for these varieties is greater than for the more traditional varieties, the variability of water depth in which the high-yield varieties are productive is much more restricted. Irrigated areas are quick to adopt the high-yielding varieties. The planting of higher-yielding rice varieties in Cambodia over the past several years has contributed to an impressive increase in rice yields, especially for those with irrigation-controlled flooding. In particular, rice yields have increased from an average rate of 1.25 tons per hectare during the 1985 to 1986 harvest seasons to 1.98 tons per hectare during the 1998 to 1999 agricultural harvests (Ministry of Agriculture [MOA], 2008a). The majority of this increase was obtained in areas where farmers were able to control water levels with irrigation flooding. Farmers attempting to harvest rice by means of rainwater alone, are very reluctant to adopt the high-yield rice varieties even when the seed stock is provided free of charge by a donating organization. Farmers who live in marginal lands near the Tonle Sap, however, continue to struggle with the decision to plant high-yield rice varieties. These farmers choose between a more stable and lower-yield rice variety and a less stable, higher-yield one. For many, the risk of planting the higher-yield varieties is too great to bear.

Rice yields for every province in Cambodia have been measured directly (by the achieved yields per hectare during the wet seasons) by the Ministry of Agriculture since 1998. As rice yields increase, both landmine/UXO accidents and tampering incidents are likely to decrease, albeit through distinctly different channels.

Landmine/UXO accidents are likely to decrease as rice yields increase due to the fact that an increase in rice yields does not require as much land usage. When farmers are able to select which land to cultivate, marginal lands known or assumed to be contaminated with ordnance are selected last. Farmers without access to higher-yield rice varieties inevitably utilize more land. More specifically, farmers will use land to a point where the marginal benefits from use are equal to the marginal costs.[7] Farmers will expand crop production, striking a balance between the relative ease of cultivation and perceived ordnance risks. Following the concepts of marginal analysis, implementing strategies of maximizing land usage in environments containing landmine-related ordnance would increase the likelihood that landmine/UXO accidents would occur.

As agricultural vulnerability decreases following the increased yields of rice, tampering behavior is likely to diminish. Agricultural vulnerability is largely influenced by productive capacities within the agrarian process. As food requirements are better met through people experiencing higher yields of rice per hectare, tampering activities are less likely to occur. The production of a greater amount of rice per hectare is therefore likely to diminish tampering.

Province-level annual rice yields were obtained from the Ministry of Agriculture's wet-season yield tables. Rice yields reflect the gross tonnage of rice produced per hectare. The wet season in Cambodia, sometimes referred to as the monsoon season, occurs between May and October. Dry-season yield estimates are not used because many of the provinces record a value of 0. This figure is not actually representative of yields obtained but rather reflects that rice was not planted. Because of the confusion in interpreting results, only wet-season yields are considered. Natural limitations exist, therefore, that exclude actual dry-season rice yields from the observation unit. In spite of this perceived limitation, farmers typically plant the same varieties of rice in the dry season as they do in the wet season. If farmers do plant diverse rice varieties in different seasons, it is likely that this practice takes place uniformly throughout the country. Following this same logic, if standard yields of rice are lower during dry-season harvest cycles, it is most likely that any deviation from the mean would occur at a standardized rate among all provinces observed. Measuring rice yields by considering only wet-season rice yields, therefore, probably mirrors the complete agricultural cycle image.

4.2.3. Crop Diversification

Among all agricultural land in Cambodia, 84.4% is allocated to rice cultivation (MOA, 2008a). Although rice is produced in every province, significant geographic and temporal variations of rice production exist among them.

Labor requirements of rice cultivation are higher than those of other crops.[8] Where traditional plowing techniques are used, the methods of production are even more labor and time intensive in comparison to tractor tilling.[9] In addition, areas characterized by extensive rice cultivation via traditional techniques also typically suffer from a dearth of fertilizers and subsequently experience lower yields. Farmers expand cultivation into increasingly risky areas in an effort to produce sufficient rice to meet their needs. This behavior leads to the occurrence of landmine/UXO accidents.

While rice cultivation is more labor intensive than any other type of farming, there exist wide variations in labor requirements depending on the method of plowing. Land appropriate for the cultivation of rice is composed of slightly acidic clay. Clay hardens with time and must be softened before the rice seed can be planted. Wealthier areas of Cambodia have been able to adopt the use of tractors and advanced plows, which helps to significantly decrease the time necessary to prepare the soil for planting. Those who cannot afford these advanced methods rely upon the traditional single plow pulled by buffalo.[10] Areas with a greater proportion of agricultural land used for rice cultivation rely more heavily upon the traditional methods involving buffalo and the single plow (MOA, 2008b).

Areas with high proportions of rice cultivation suffer from lower average rice yields, subsequently increasing agricultural vulnerability and impacting landmine/UXO incidents. As more land is allocated to rice, the yield decreases. For every 10% increase in planting of rice, the marginal yield drops by 2.2%.[11] This decrease in yield is explained in part by the lack of fertilizer in areas predominantly planting rice. Lower yields of rice then force farmers to seek new land to farm in the next agricultural season. When yields are too low, farmers even risk planting on landmine-contaminated land. In summary, rice monoculture raises the risk of landmine/UXO incidents as a result of a combination of factors including extensive use of labor, buffalo-driven tilling, low yields, and low fertilizer use.

Lack of crop diversification also raises farmers' economic exposure, which may force them to undertake activities that subject them to landmine/UXO hazards. Crop diversification spreads out the risk involved in producing agricultural products. If one crop fails because of insufficient rain, it is likely others survive the drought. Unfortunately, not all Cambodian farmers are capable of diversifying their crops due to insufficient financial backing, inadequate skills and training, and geographic variations in soil conditions.

I use the proportion of farmland allocated to rice cultivation at the province level as a landmine/UXO risk factor. Information regarding rice proportions was compiled from data gathered by provincial heads throughout Cambodia and compared to statistics obtained from the Ministry of Agriculture in Phnom Penh.

Crop diversification is measured directly with no process of transformation or proxy estimation. It should be understood, however, that stated values of rice-allocated land are compared to the aggregated hectares planted with some type of agricultural product. Hectares not planted are not included in the stated figure. It is conceivable, therefore, that the proportion of rice cultivation could increase from one year to the next while the total number of hectares planted with rice diminished. This reality should be kept in mind when interpreting results.

4.2.4. Natural Disasters

Natural disasters—droughts, floods, and insect infestation—can destroy rice crops. Floods destroy crops whenever the water gets deeper than the maximum allowable depth for the specific rice variety planted. Floods primarily occur in areas where excess water cannot be drained from fields or in areas lacking irrigation controls. High-yield rice varieties have a smaller bandwidth of acceptable water depth that will allow the crop to mature, and they are most often planted in areas with irrigation-control mechanisms. The majority of Cambodian farmers (nearly 80%), however, do not use irrigation, leaving them susceptible to flooding.

Each variety of rice exhibits unique qualities of durability and resilience. Even the strongest varieties of rice, however, eventually wither and die without water. Irrigation mechanisms redirect water from major water sources to the desiccated rice fields. Absent irrigation, farmers are left to perform traditional "rain-beckoning" practices in hopes of convincing a deity to deliver the much-needed rain to their rice fields. Droughts can affect rice fields throughout the year but are especially prevalent during the dry season.

Natural disasters also include insect infestation, including any organism or microbe with the ability to reduce or completely eradicate a rice harvest. These pests can include birds, insects, rodents, and pathogens. On average, only 0.57% of the rice crop has been lost to insect infestation, a figure far below traditional levels of damage caused by floods and droughts. Insect infestation may be prevented by pesticides and, not surprisingly, areas most susceptible to insect infestation are those that cannot afford pesticides. Specifically, areas at greatest risk of losing crops to insect infestation are also the areas not able to plant rice in the dry season. Impoverishment leading to lack of flood-control mechanisms also prevents farmers from purchasing pesticides.

The majority of Cambodians live at or near a level of minimum subsistence, making the loss of rice crops to natural disasters a reality with severe consequences, forcing people undertake activities that, in turn, subject them landmine/UXO hazards. The proportion of rice crops destroyed by natural causes has been recorded by the Ministry of Agriculture since 1998. In the empirical analysis, I will estimate the impact of the rice crop lost on landmine-related incidents as a landmine/UXO risk factor.

Three basic categories of natural disaster have been tracked in Cambodia's agrarian sector: droughts, floods, and insect infestation. Droughts are experienced when crops do not receive sufficient quantities of water to produce a harvest. In contrast, floods occur when a crop receives too much water for too long, drowning the possibility of a harvest taking place. Lastly, insect infestation occurs when any form of pathogen, insect, bird, or pest diminishes the productive capacity of a rice harvest.

Landmine/UXO accidents and tampering incidents are both likely to increase with increased proportions of rice crops lost to natural disasters. Natural disasters destroying a portion of a season's harvest increase the likelihood of accidents because marginal lands, which are often contaminated with landmine-related ordnance, are now utilized in an attempt to regain some lost crop. Tampering is also likely to increase with the onset of natural disasters because each form of natural disaster increases the severity of agricultural vulnerability and gives rise to an economic incentive to engage in tampering activities.

Droughts and floods increase agricultural vulnerability. Farmers may choose to plant more crops following the loss of crops to these forms of natural disaster. Land chosen for planting additional crops in the presence of a drought or flood is less desirable than land initially planted and sometimes involves landmine-contaminated plots. Whether or not farmers choose to plant additional crops in marginal lands, food-foraging takes place in an effort to replace lost crops, and the crossing and utilization of landmine-contaminated land becomes a greater possibility. Although many know of the risks associated with foraging in contaminated areas, this option is more feasible than the alternative. Landmine-related accidents will therefore increase following the occurrence of a drought or flood.

As droughts and floods occur, tampering activities are seen as a temporary solution to the vulnerability being experienced. Farmers opting to search for scrap metal can usually do so in relatively close proximity to their home farms. The only situation that would prevent tampering behavior from taking place would be the advent of a great proportion of farms experiencing flooding in close proximity to each other. Because flooding typically occurs on a small scale, with an average of 4.1% of crops lost to flooding in a typical year, metal scrapping and the tampering that follows need only avoid the specific flooded hectares.

The proportion of rice fields destroyed by insect infestation is also positively correlated with landmine/UXO accidents and tampering incidents. Insect infestation is not highly correlated with droughts or floods; it is a unique natural disaster influencing situations of agricultural vulnerability. Following the loss of rice crops to insects, landmine-related accidents increase because marginal lands often contaminated with ordnance are more likely to be utilized in an effort to make up for the lost crops. Landmine/UXO tampering incidents are also more likely to increase because with the loss of crops, farmers are subject to a greater degree of agricultural vulnerability, so they seek metal to sell in order to avoid starvation.

Information concerning natural disasters exists in raw form represented by the number of hectares destroyed by droughts, floods, and insect infestation. Data are complete for each province of Cambodia between 1999 and 2006. These data were transformed to represent the proportion of the rice crop destroyed by each disaster measure. Each natural disaster measure is individually recognized when performing econometric testing. No apparent limitation regarding these directly measured variables is evident.

4.2.5. Substitutes for Rice

When rice harvests are meager or insufficient to meet people's needs, other food sources are relied upon. A greater number of alternatives to rice reduces agricultural vulnerability. Crop substitutes for rice in Cambodia include banana, black pepper, cashew, coconut, coffee, custard apple, cassava, durian, guava, jack fruit, jute, longan, mango, maize, milk fruit, mung bean, orange, palm oil, palm tree, peanut, pineapple, rambutan, sapodilla, sesame, soya bean, sugar cane, sweet potato, and tobacco. Another substitute for rice is fish. Spilling from the enormous Tonle Sap into thousands of smaller waterways are a recorded 490 species of fish. Some provinces in Cambodia have direct access to water channels, and others do not. Each year, the average Cambodian consumes 20 kilograms of fish. As a last resort, Cambodians facing rice shortages slaughter their working livestock. Buffalo used in traditional field tilling can provide reprieve from starvation. It is likely, therefore, that a province with a large supply of livestock would experience a smaller risk of agricultural vulnerability in the short term.

Each of these substitutes for rice represents the ability of people to receive sustenance when rice supplies are meager. Accordingly, a negative relationship exists between availability of nonrice food and landmine/UXO accidents and tampering incidents. Accidents are specifically decreased because foraging actions in unmarked and dangerous terrain are not necessary when established crop alternatives exist. As agricultural vulnerability is decreased in areas with rice substitutes, tampering activities also decline. Substitutes for rice are measured as an aggregate of other crops, and separate indices exist for fish and buffalo. Summary statistics for all variables used in the following tests can be observed in Table 4.1.

4.3. Empirical Model

This section tests the hypothesis that economic need experienced in the agricultural sector affects landmine/UXO accidents and tampering incidents. As in the previous chapter, dependent variables are the landmine/UXO accident, landmine/UXO tampering, and the pooled incidents measured annually at the province level. Independent variables are net rice

TABLE 4.1. Dependent and Independent Variable Summary Statistics.

	MINIMUM	MEAN	MAXIMUM	STANDARD DEVIATION
Accidents	0	0.86	19.2	2.86
Tampering	0	0.75	15.58	1.8
Incidents	0	1.61	31.17	4.43
Net Rice Supply*	0.005	0.168	0.519	0.098
Supply of Water (percent)	0 (31.4 percent of cases)	12.6	73.3	25
Rice Variety Yields*	1.04	1.86	3.68	0.45
Crop Diversification (percent)	2.1	86.3	99.5	16.3
Floods (percent)	0	4.1	28.7	6.7
Droughts (percent)	0	3.1	67.9	7.4
Insect Infestation (percent)	0	0.1	26.3	2.5
Substitutes to Rice**	0	0.137	1.312	0.217
Fish**	0	0.022	0.226	0.033
Buffalo***	0.004	0.5	3.1	0.555

Note. *Data in relation to tons per hectare. **Data in relation to kilos per population. ***Data in relation to population.

production per capita; supply of water; rice yields; crop diversification; crops lost to droughts, floods, and insect infestation; nonrice crop output per capita; fish per capita; and buffalo per capita. They are represented as follows:

$$Y_i = \beta_{0i} + \beta_{1i}R + \beta_{2i}W + \beta_{3i}RY + \beta_{4i}C + \beta_{5i}NDD + \beta_{6i}NDF + \beta_{7i}NDI + \beta_{8i}NR + \beta_{9i}F + \beta_{10i}B + e_i \tag{4.1}$$

where i = Incident, A = Accident, and T = Tampering. R is net rice production per capita, W represents supply of water, RY represents rice yields, C is the share of land allocated to rice cultivation, NDD represents natural disasters in the form of droughts, NDF represents natural disasters in the form of floods, NDI is equivalent to natural disasters in the form of insect infestation, NR represents nonrice per capita, F stands for fish per capita, and B represents buffalo per capita.

Landmine/UXO incident statistics were obtained from the Cambodian Mine Victim Information System (CMVIS, 2008). Accidents and tampering incidents have been separated according to stated activities at the time of incident occurrence as discussed in the previous chapters. Incidents comprise the combination of landmine/UXO accidents and tampering incidents. Accident, tampering, and incident rates are stated as population figures per population of 10,000 influenced by each incident category. Population statistics were obtained from the National Institute of Statistics (NIS, 2004b). Information regarding dependent variables was obtained from the Ministry of Agriculture (MOA, 2008b). Estimations are carried out for a panel of 24 provinces over 8 years (1999–2006).

One shortcoming of the study should be pointed out: Data for independent variables in both the Otdar Meanchey and Pailin provinces between 1998 and 2000 do not exist. Neither of these provinces existed at the time of the analysis and therefore cannot be included in the analysis. Accordingly, panel data adjustments using unbalanced estimators were included in regressions.

4.4. Regression Results

Panel estimates of the impact of agricultural variables on landmine-related incidents, accidents, and tampering are reported in Table 4.2.

4.4.1. Landmine/UXO Incident Findings

The first column in Table 4.2 shows four statistically significant agricultural vulnerability measures. Most significant in regard to both statistical relevance and size of coefficient is the impact the supply of water has on incidents. Due to the fact that the water supply variable proxies agricultural vulnerability by comparing crops produced during the dry season

TABLE 4.2. Regression Output of Agricultural Vulnerability on Landmine/UXO Incidents, Accidents and Tampering.

	Incidents	Accidents	Tampering
Net Rice Per Capita	-5.19	-1.19	-4
	(3.18)*	-2.23	(1.99)**
Supply of Water	-6.07	-1.56	-4.51
	(1.31)***	(0.92)*	(0.82)***
Rice Yields	0.26	-0.39	0.66
	-0.38	(0.27)*	(0.24)***
Rice-Specific Crop	-0.02	0.05	-0.07
	-0.02	(0.01)***	(0.01)***
Droughts	2.27	0.41	1.86
	(1.61)*	-1.13	(1.01)**
Floods	1.16	-0.48	1.64
	-1.74	-1.22	(1.09)*
Insect Infestation	7.68	2.9	4.79
	-5.94	-4.17	-3.72
Nonrice Per Capita	-2.09	-0.68	-1.41
	(1.35)*	-0.95	(0.85)*
Fish Per Capita	-0.18	0.44	-0.61
	-5.47	-3.85	-3.43
Buffalo Per Capita	0.15	0.12	0.02
	-0.67	-0.47	-0.42
constant	4.83	-1.96	6.79
	-2.1	-1.48	-1.32
R-sq (within)	0.19	0.16	0.35
R-sq (between)	0.04	0.42	0.36
R-sq (overall)	0.04	0.24	0.31
sigma_u	4.85	3.93	1.53
sigma_e	1.29	0.9	0.81
F-test	0	0	0

Note. Standard errors in parenthesis, Number of Observations = 188, Number of Groups = 24. *Significant at the 10 percent level, **Significant at the 5 percent level, ***Significant at the 1 percent level.

to crops produced during the wet season, the findings indicate areas with a greater supply of water have fewer landmine/UXO incidents. This finding is statistically significant at the 1% level. In fact, for every 1%

increase in dry-season rice crops relative to the overall rice production, landmine/UXO incidents decrease by a rate of .61 per 10,000. These findings should not be interpreted to suggest that Cambodia should shift toward a dry-season rice crop; rather, these findings advocate for a more consistent annual crop.

Given that the major limitation to annual planting is the supply of water, increasing the supply of water would most certainly increase aggregate crops, which would in turn decrease agricultural vulnerabilities and, hence, landmine/UXO incidents. Again, as is indicated by the results of the regression, increasing the proportion of rice crops realized during the dry season would reduce the rate of landmine/UXO incidents experienced in Cambodia. Policies that could aid in this effort may consist of water right policies, water transfer strategies, the construction of flood-controlled irrigation channels, and education concerning water storage techniques.

Net rice per capita, droughts, and nonrice per capita are all statistically significant variables influencing landmine/UXO incident rates at the 10% level. Net rice per capita and nonrice per capita are both negatively correlated with the landmine/UXO incident rate, whereas droughts are positively correlated. While these variables are similar in that they share the same degree of statistical significance, coefficient strengths and policy approaches are vastly distinct between them.

Net rice per capita is correlated with tampering at a 5% level of significance. In spite of the magnitude of the beta coefficient and the strength of the statistical correlation, policy makers should target this variable with careful consideration. Increasing net rice per capita values by even a seemingly infinitesimal level could prove a colossal task. While attempting to increase per-capita rice yields can be approached a myriad of ways, most are likely to prove ineffective. For example, policy targeting the use of higher-yield rice varieties, even when providing seed stock by direct subsidization, has not historically proven successful in this country because of the increased crop failure risk inherent with high-yield varieties. In conjunction with increased rates of crop failure, farmers weigh risk against potential gain and nearly always determine that increased rates of risk associated with higher-yield rice varieties cannot be borne. It is more likely that an increase in rice per capita could be accomplished by targeting an indirect measure such as the supply of water.

Recognition of the impact both the net rice per capita and the supply of water have on reducing the landmine/UXO incident rates directs a clear path for policy recommendation. More specifically, net rice per capita is directly tied to the ability to produce rice in the dry season. Agricultural policy targeted at the reduction of ordnance incidents should be designed in an effort to increase dry-season cultivation practices. While this would require an increased supply of water, the end objective of reducing accidents and tampering could be accomplished both directly and indirectly by approaching the issue from this angle. Policy targeting an increase in net rice yields through a direct subsidy of high-yield seed stock would prove inferior to policy that increased net rice yields indirectly by establishing irrigation mechanisms. Policy makers should, therefore, recognize the link between the water supply using irrigation and the ability to increase net rice yields per capita.

When a portion of a harvest is destroyed by drought, landmine/UXO incidents increase. The magnitude by which droughts impact the overall landmine/UXO rate, however, are below those of net rice per capita and the supply of water. More precisely, a substantial loss of crops due to droughts at a level of 10% would lead to an increased landmine/UXO incident rate of .227 per population of 10,000. In other words, a population would have to be near 40,000 and experience a substantial 10% loss of crop due to drought in order to experience an increase of one landmine/UXO incident. Policy instruments that would help to prevent droughts are also tied to irrigation measures. More exactly, if a province experiences a surge in irrigation channels, droughts will decrease, generating a reduction in the landmine/UXO incident rate. Policy focusing on introducing irrigation on a massive scale, therefore, has feedback effects through various measures.

The last variable reflected as being statistically significant in conjunction with the landmine/UXO incident calculation is in regard to nonrice production values per capita. As nonrice production increases by 0.1 ton per person per year, landmine/UXO incident rates fall by .21 people per population of 10,000. In accordance with the policy recommendation from the previous three variables, as irrigation mechanisms are put in place, nonrice yields per capita will increase. Targeting the implementation of irrigation controls, therefore, impacts each variable considered relevant to the overall picture of landmine/UXO incidents in a desirable direction.

4.4.2. Landmine/UXO Accident Findings

While insights have been gained examining the relationship between several measures of agricultural vulnerability and landmine/UXO incident rates, separating incidents into categories of accidents and tampering provides deeper insights and more appropriate policy directives. Three statistically significant variables exist relative to landmine/UXO accidents. Specifically, the water supply, rice yields, and rice-specific crop proportions are all variables with statistically significant correlations with the landmine/UXO accident rate.

If one recalls that the supply of water is measured in proxy by the proportion of rice-specific crop from dry-season periods, interpretation of this variable becomes more simplistic. Higher proportions of rice produced in the dry season indicate a greater supply of water. As the percentage of the total rice crop produced during the dry season increases by 10%, landmine/UXO accidents decrease by a rate of 0.16 per population of 10,000. This result is statistically significant at the 10% level. Following this finding, it would be worthwhile for policy makers to again consider implementing large-scale irrigation projects that would facilitate rice production during dry seasons.

The next statistically significant variable, incidentally also at the 10% level, measures rice yields during wet seasons. As yields of rice per hectare of rice planted increase, landmine/UXO accidents decrease. More precisely, as average rice yields increase from 1 ton per hectare to 2 tons per hectare, landmine/UXO accidents decrease by a rate of 0.39 per population of 10,000. The most obvious policy recommendation in conjunction with this finding would be to continue introducing high-yield rice varieties to Cambodian farmers. A program following this mandate should also be paired with an initiative that assists in absorbing the additional risk introduced with planting higher-yield rice varieties. A second, less obvious policy recommendation follows the established need to create a firm network of irrigation channels throughout the country. As water supplies increase, yields of rice increase because rice can be planted year-round in areas known to be uncontaminated with landmine-related ordnance.

The last statistically significant variable among all of the mentioned measures of agricultural vulnerability and the landmine/UXO accident rate relates to the percentage of of rice planted on a farmer's land. This variable is statistically significant at the 1% level, indicating a strong correlation between rice-specific crop proportions and landmine-related accidents. More directly, as rice-specific crop proportions increase by 10%, landmine/UXO accidents increase by 0.005 per population of 10,000. While perhaps this finding seems trivial, the average population among Cambodia's 26 provinces lies at 549,404, indicating that even a 1% increase in rice-specific crop proportions could increase landmine/UXO accidents by 275, a value not insignificant by any measure. Policy measures directed at reducing the landmine/UXO accident rate should, therefore, consider diversifying crops.

4.4.3. Landmine/UXO Tampering Findings

Many of the stated measures of agricultural vulnerability reflect statistically significant values in relation to landmine/UXO tampering incidents. More specifically, net rice per capita, the supply of water, rice yields, rice-specific crop percentages, droughts, floods, and nonrice per-capita yields are all correlated with landmine/UXO tampering incidents to a statistically significant degree.

As net rice per capita increases, landmine/UXO tampering incidents decrease. More exactly, as rice yields increase by 0.1 ton per person, landmine/UXO tampering rates decrease by 0.4 per population of 10,000. This result, which is statistically significant at the 5% level, shows that the majority of increase experienced in landmine/UXO incidents is within the category of tampering incidents. Increasing net rice per capita, therefore, alters incentives to seek scrap metal and should be critically considered when forming polices targeted at reducing landmine-related incidents.

As water becomes more readily available, assisting in producing more food during the dry seasons, landmine/UXO accidents, tampering incidents, and the subsequent overall incident rates fall. The majority of influence within this variable takes place within tampering incidents. As was noted when observing the overall relationship between the proportion of rice-specific crops grown during dry seasons and the landmine/UXO incident rate, a 10% increase in this value is correlated with a decrease of 0.61 per population of 10,000. Of this 0.61 per population of 10,000, the majority has been determined to be tampering—more precisely, 0.45 of the 0.61. This result is statistically significant at the 1% level. Understandably, therefore, while increasing water supplies by means of irrigation reduces the overall landmine/UXO incident rate, the majority of this influence is felt as tampering incidents fall in response to a more stable rice crop year round. This emphasizes the importance of including irrigation-targeted policy objectives within any substantial landmine/UXO reduction plan.

Both rice yields and rice-specific crop proportions prove statistically significant at the 1% level. While very strong correlations exist between both of these variables and the landmine/UXO tampering incident rate, the direction of causality is backward from what was hypothesized.

First, as rice yields increase, landmine/UXO tampering incidents also increase. While this is in contradiction to the hypothesized relationship relating agricultural vulnerability to the need to tamper, perhaps an argument of geography explains this finding. Tampering occurring in the Pailin province takes place at a high rate because former militants intentionally relocate near the border to engage in tampering before metal is sold as scrap to Thailand. The Pailin province, while experiencing high rates of tampering incidents, also specializes in nonrice production because of its high soil acidity levels. It is likely, however, that risk-taking behavior inherent in the tampering process spills over into the decision-making process involving agricultural planting. Individuals encountering high levels of risk during tampering activities are more likely to take on risk when planting seed stock.

Next, as the proportion of crop planted as rice increases, tampering incidents decrease. This finding is in contradiction to suggested logical relationships between these two variables, again at the hand of geographic idiosyncrasies. The Pailin province, once again, proves an outlier in this example. Rice-specific crop percentages are very low in the Pailin province, again because of the acidity levels of the soil. In spite of this reality, Pailin experiences one of the highest tampering incident counts. Expatriate relocation, in conjunction with the common border between Cambodia and Thailand, is likely to explain this phenomenon.

Droughts also have a direct and statistically significant (at the 0.5% level) impact on landmine/UXO tampering. For every 1% of rice crop destroyed by droughts, tampering incident rates increase by 0.02 per population of 10,000. Droughts can most effectively be reduced by introducing irrigation into the agricultural process.

When floods drown rice crops in Cambodia, landmine/UXO tampering rates increase. Statically significant at the 5% level, for every 1% increase in flooded rice paddies, tampering incidents increase by 0.016 per population of 10,000. Again, the target mechanism whereby policy makers can curb the impact of natural disasters and subsequently reduce landmine-related casualties is simply a function of implementing flood-controlled irrigation structures.

The last statistically significant variable contributing to the landmine/UXO tampering incident rate is specific to the nonrice yields of produce per capita. As nonrice values increase in magnitude, landmine/UXO tampering rates fall. More precisely, for every 0.1 ton per capita increase in nonrice product, landmine/UXO incidents fall by a rate of 0.14 per population of 10,000. Diversifying the agricultural production of food commodities in Cambodia should, therefore, again be considered a relevant policy approach in reducing landmine-related incidents.

4.5. Conclusions and Recommendations

Comparing factors of agricultural vulnerability to the observed landmine/UXO accident and tampering rates has made clear several pertinent correlations. These findings have helped to substantiate the hypotheses surrounding the causes of landmine/UXO incidents. The implementation of policy directed at reducing landmine/UXO incidents must, therefore, consider the impacts of agricultural vulnerability. Additionally, policy simply targeted at landmine/UXO incidents fails to recognize the significance of each incident category. As has been shown, several measures of agricultural vulnerability significantly impact accidents and tampering incidents without being reflected in the aggregate measure of landmine/UXO incidents. More precisely, following a surge in agricultural vulnerability, landmine/UXO accidents are not always impacted in the same way as landmine/UXO tampering incidents. Importantly, therefore, policy makers should concern themselves with reducing landmine/UXO incidents on two separate fronts: accidents and tampering incidents. Section 4.5.1 will elaborate on recommendations for policy makers with regard to landmine/UXO accidents, and Section 4.5.2 will do the same with regard to landmine/UXO tampering incidents.

4.5.1. Policy to Reduce Landmine/UXO Accidents

First, in regard to landmine-related accidents, several relationships are evident. In order to have a desirable impact on the landmine/UXO accident rate, policy makers must target increasing the supply of water to fields, increasing rice yields, and diversifying crops to provide a balance between rice and nonrice production. All of these policy instruments are important regarding the direct effects they can have on reducing the landmine/UXO accident rate.

In order to provide sufficient water to Cambodia's crops, especially during the dry seasons, it is first obligatory to structure operable irrigation systems throughout the country. The ability to control water levels is crucial in increasing dry-season rice hectares planted and harvested. Once a stable irrigation infrastructure is in place, dry-season yields can also be improved upon by focusing on high-yield rice varieties and the use of fertilizers. Providing a system by which farmers can access water in sufficient abundance and redirect overflows to appropriate areas is an essential element in eliminating agricultural vulnerabilities experienced in Cambodia.

Increasing rice yields requires the adaptation of higher-yield rice varieties and the use of fertilizers in the crop-preparation stages. Each of these issues has an obvious obstacle to overcome. Farmers make decisions not to plant the higher-yield rice varieties because of the increased harvest-failure risk associated with doing so. Because higher-yield rice varieties require a more stable supply of water, it is again requisite that flood-control irrigation be in place before farmers will decide to plant entire harvests in the higher-yield varieties. Fertilizers are often not used because they are expensive. In the short run, if policy makers wish to increase rice yields through the use of fertilizers, direct subsidization will probably be necessary. After experiencing several harvest cycles producing in sufficient abundance, it is likely that farmers can sell surplus produce and then afford fertilizers.

Diversifying crops will require training for many farmers. The practice of rice farming is traditionally learned from parents, limiting the knowledge of planting and harvesting techniques to a familial body of knowledge. Additionally, farmers typically lack access to seeds to plant for other food products. Policy makers should, therefore, consider providing an initial seed stock and basic training about planting and harvesting techniques in order to help diversify crops.

4.5.2. Policy to Reduce Landmine/UXO Tampering

Second, in regard to landmine-related tampering, arguments have been made regarding increasing net rice per-capita yields, increasing the supply of water to rice fields (especially during the dry seasons), increasing rice yields, diversifying the production of food commodities, decreasing the impact of droughts and floods, and increasing nonrice per-capita yields. Policy directed at each of these measures of agricultural vulnerability can help to decrease the landmine/UXO tampering rates in Cambodia. Increasing net rice yields per capita critically hinges on having sufficient supplies of water and the adoption of high-yield rice varieties. Both of these critical policies were mentioned in reducing the landmine/UXO accident rate and remain foundational to reducing the landmine/UXO tampering rate.

Diversifying crops is critical in regard to reducing both accident and tampering incidents. In addition to the aforementioned policies involving subsidizing seed stock and providing training, it is also critical that the nonrice products increase in per-capita yields so as to reduce in the landmine/UXO tampering rates. Finding alternatives to rice-specific products appears critical in reducing agricultural vulnerability and the associated tampering behavior. Policy makers can, therefore, direct farmers to plant nonrice products that provide the best substitution for rice in terms of productivity per hectare.

Landmine/UXO tampering incidents are also highly correlated with droughts and floods. Fortunately, many of the problems caused by excessive periods of rain and no rain can be solved with simplistic measures of irrigation. Channeling water to and from the Tonle Sap, the major waterway in Cambodia, can avoid many of the problems inherent with droughts and flooding.

Policy makers can use statistics from the Ministry of Agriculture to predict trends in landmine/UXO accidents and tampering incidents. While important separations have been made between these two categories, agriculturally based policy recommendations for both accidents and tampering are similar in nature. The following four basic policy propositions will lead to decreased rates of landmine/UXO accidents and tampering incidents:

1. Create a sustainable irrigation-based infrastructure specifically suited to provide water to all parts of Cambodia in all seasons, and limit the impact of floods and droughts.
2. Implement the use of high-yield rice varieties throughout Cambodia, initially by means of direct subsidization and donor acceptance of harvest risk.
3. Determine which nonrice agricultural products are best suited as substitutions for rice and introduce these products to farmers.
4. Diversify crops by providing an initial endowment of seed stock and specific planting and harvesting training to farmers.

Each of these targeted propositions will come at a cost. Creating an infrastructure that will facilitate flood-controlled irrigation throughout the country is an enormous and expensive task. Subsidizing high-yield rice varieties and shifting the risk of crop failure to the donor requires, first, a donor. Discovering and shifting to a nonrice substitute will involve substantial research and modification of traditional practices. Diversifying crops with an initial endowment of seed stock will necessitate a substantial amount of farmer training and come at a cost of decreased economies of scale.

Cost determination regarding each of these policy propositions is absolutely critical. Prior to implementing policy, it must be known that the benefits from the enactment of policy are greater than the costs. The benefits from a reduction in landmine/UXO incidents are substantial over time, but the costs must be borne in advance. It is not requisite, however, for Mine Action to take on the entire cost of implementing strategies stemming from these findings. Mine Action practitioners should use this information—now statistically delineated and demarcated—to advocate for change in a direction that would facilitate a reduction in landmine/ UXO incidents.

ENDNOTES

1. Stated figure from 2005. In 1999, 76.5% of Cambodia's workforce was engaged in agrarian labor. This number fell to 71.2% by 2005, with the decreased proportion of agrarian laborers accounted for in the service and industry sectors.
2. This number is vastly different in rural and urban areas. Specifically, rice in some rural areas accounts for more than 90% of caloric intake and in some urban areas less than 40%.
3. Marginal lands are often contaminated with landmines/UXO.
4. This figure is standard across time and space for the purposes of this analysis. It is likely that there are distinctions between the amount of seed required between low- and higher-yielding varieties, but no data exist to substantiate this claim. It is also likely that postharvest losses are not consistent across time and space, but differentiation is not recorded and therefore cannot be used in this analysis.
5. This number, again, is likely to be differentiated in specific areas focusing on higher-yielding human-consumption varieties. The Ministry of Agriculture recognizes that this difference exists but states that it is small enough to not be concerned with. Best guess estimates from the director of the Ministry estimate a 2% to 3% differentiation.
6. Figure from 2005. Efforts to increase irrigation in Cambodia have commenced. Specifically, only 12% of Cambodia's rice fields were fed with irrigation as recently as 1998.
7. It is likely that the calculation of marginal costs in the case where land may contain ordnance is a perceived cost rather than an actual cost.
8. The Ministry of Agriculture estimates that 3,200 man hours are expended for every metric ton of rice produced in Cambodia. This figure is more than double the required labor input of any other crop grown in the country.
9. Tractor tilling speeds up the land preparation stages involving initial excavation, leveling processes, dike building, sluice gate creation, and fertilizer tilling.
10. Tractor tilling is not only faster but also requires fewer sweeps across the soil to till it sufficiently for planting. Understandably, tractor tilling requires less interaction with the soil.
11. This information was compiled from datasets obtained from the Ministry of Agriculture in Phnom Penh. Unless otherwise noted, information has come from this source.

Chapter 5

The Price of Scrap Metal and Landmine/UXO Tampering Behavior

> It is the random nature of large-scale mine dissemination that makes mines so damaging to rural communities, but certain groups and individuals within those communities are critically vulnerable.
>
> —McGrath, 1994

5.1. Introduction

Explosive remnants of war speckle Cambodia's landscape. Hidden beneath rice field banks, sitting dormant on hillside slopes, and entangled in the roots of kapok trees, residual landmines and unexploded ordnance (UXO) exist in numbers greater than Cambodia's population. Some discover landmine-related ordnance accidentally while taking an unfortunate step in a rice field, while others intentionally seek postwar scrap in order to sell ordnance components. Both accidental and tampering incidents result in injury or death.

Tampering has dominated Cambodia's landmine/UXO incidents ever since 2000.[1] As China engaged in rapid industrialization, its traditional metal exports to Cambodia's neighbor, Thailand, came to a standstill. Metal supply shortages in Thailand raised the price of metal substantially. Cambodians responded to expanding demand by selling metal to Thailand, metal often recovered from landmines and UXO.

This chapter tests the hypothesis that landmine/UXO tampering incidents respond to the price of metal. While this hypothesis is proposed by others (Moyes, 2004), it has never been tested due to the lack of a metal price record on the Cambodia–Thailand border.[2] I constructed a price series that facilitates the testing of the proposed hypothesis. If the price of metal is indeed a critical factor, then policy makers can make use of this information in their efforts to reduce tampering.

In this chapter, I first discuss the tampering behavior. Section 5.3 describes the supply chain from the original discovery of ordnance to the final sale across international borders. Section 5.4 introduces the border metal price record I compiled in Cambodia. Section 5.5 presents the empirical model. Section 5.6 discusses empirical findings. Finally, Section 5.7 concludes by offering policy recommendations.

5.2. Tampering

I define tampering as intentional engagement with landmines/UXO in order to benefit economically from the sale, transfer, or use of it. I am able to measure tampering in a narrower sense in empirical work, however. Official records reveal only the tampering incidents resulting in an injury or fatality and therefore miss all cases where the latter are avoided.[3] Nevertheless, assuming there is a direct relationship between all tampering and tampering that resulted in injury or death, the investigation carried out in this chapter is of use.

While tampering is currently considered synonymous with UXO incidents within ordnance examination paradigms, this definition ignores the incentives that drive behavior. Ultimately, an examination of incentives can prove quite useful because policies target incentives. The current policies targeting a reduction in tampering are inaccurately consigning all UXO incidents to a tampering classification while at the same time ignoring landmine-specific tampering episodes. Accordingly, tampering episodes have been distinguished from accidental episodes according to postincident activity responses.

Scrap metal is collected across Cambodia and sold to Thailand and Vietnam,[4] where the metal is melted, reformed into rebar, and then sold back to Cambodia.[5] Metal scrappers exist in every district of Cambodia. Scrapping for metal requires nothing more than a rudimentary metal detector, a digging device, and a container to collect the metal fragments discovered. Metal scrappers are not exclusively searching for landmines or UXO, but they inevitably discover landmines/UXO (henceforth *ordnance*) in their pursuit of metal. Typical nonordnance scrap metal includes eroded farm equipment fragments, nails, pop cans, building frame shavings, wires, temple remnants, wheel-band parcels, door hinges, bottle caps, coins, chain links, and silverware. After many years of mining and carpet bombing, however, there also exists a large supply of ordnance. In addition to being plentiful, the metal encasing of ordnance is attractive to scrappers because it usually yields a substantial weight of metal when compared to other metal discoveries. In March of 2003, metal scrappers in the Svay Rieng province, for instance, reported a typical daily find of less than 1 kilogram of nonordnance scrap. The minimum weight of the metal casing of an ordnance parcel, however, is more than 1 kilogram. Comparative weights between nonordnance and ordnance scrap, therefore, suggest a strong incentive to scrap ordnance. The risk, of course, is that the ordnance may be live and may explode after recovery.

The Cambodian government has undertaken a massive campaign to educate the population about the risks of tampering. Mine-risk education has permeated every district of Cambodia, portraying the riskiness of tampering activities in various media formats. The Cambodian Mine/UXO Action Authority (CMAA) has announced strict penalties for engaging in tampering activities. In spite of the well-known physical risks and punitive measures, however, tampering persists because it provides a livelihood to poor people who have few economic alternatives.

Figure 5.1 illustrates the geographic distribution of tampering incidents across districts over the 2000 to 2005 time period. The highest concentration of tampering incidents on a per-capita basis occurs in northwestern districts neighboring Thailand, where the bulk of scrap metal transactions take place. In contrast, most of the UXO (which is most often sought in tampering processes[6]) originates in the eastern half of Cambodia, closer to Vietnam, a consequence of the extensive carpet bombing during the US–Vietnam war.

In spite of this fact, the majority of metal-trade transactions take place with Thailand. These observations suggest two points. First, the observed tampering incidents are geographically widespread because ordnance may be transported long distances between its discovery and final sale. According to the CMVIS statistics for the observed years, 81% of the districts in Cambodia experienced tampering incidents. Second and more important, the primary direction of the transportation is to northwestern Cambodia. This dominant flow of scrap metal is the outcome of the higher price of scrap metal on the Thai border in comparison with the Vietnam border.

Expansion of the scrap metal trade between Cambodia and Thailand has taken place following massive industrialization efforts on the part of China starting in the early 1990s. As domestic demand for metal in China increased, metal exports from China were reduced, causing Thailand to experience an intense metal shortage. The price of metal in Thailand increased. Cambodians responded to the price incentive. The Thai demand for metal has remained substantially higher than that of Vietnam to the east, providing an established metal price offering in Thailand higher than that of Cambodia's eastern neighbor, Vietnam.

Vietnam historically has not relied on imports of metal from China to the same degree Thailand has. According to the National Bureau of Statistics in China, metal exports to Vietnam averaged only 31% of those of Thailand between 1970 and 2008 (NIS, 2007).

Tampering activities are subject to seasonal conditions. Figure 5.2 reports monthly variations in tampering and compares dry- and wet-season

Figure 5.1. Landmine/UXO Tampering Incidents in Cambodia (2000–2007).

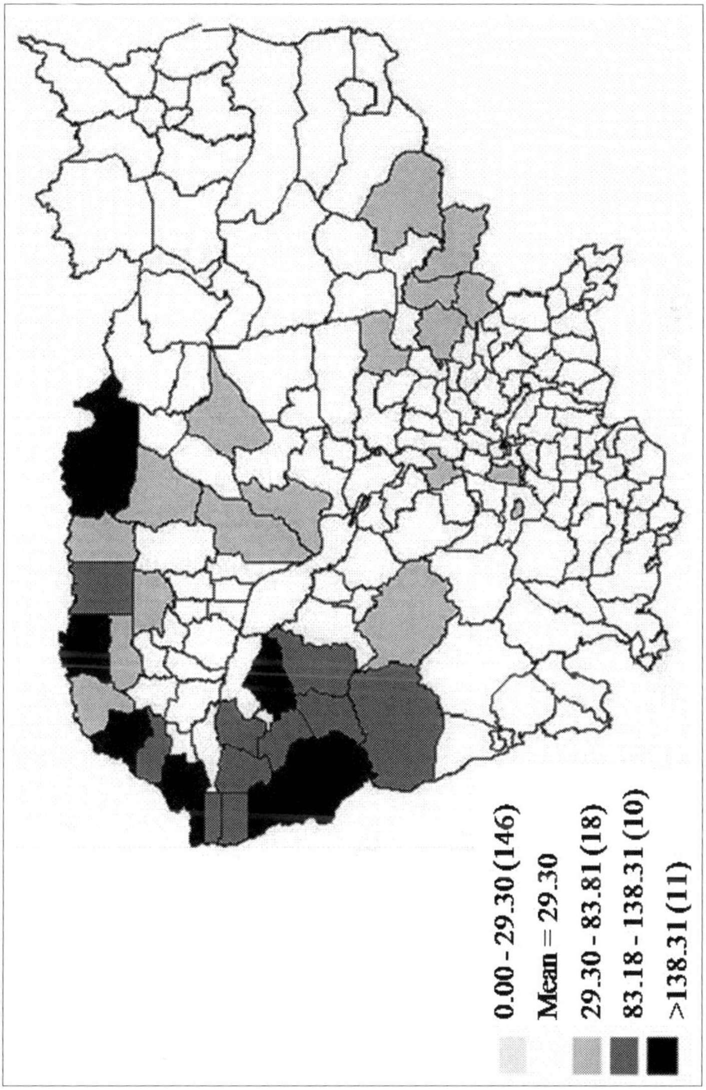

Notes. Incidents per 10,000.

FIGURE 5.2. Monthly Tampering Incident Counts Comparing Dry and Wet Seasons.

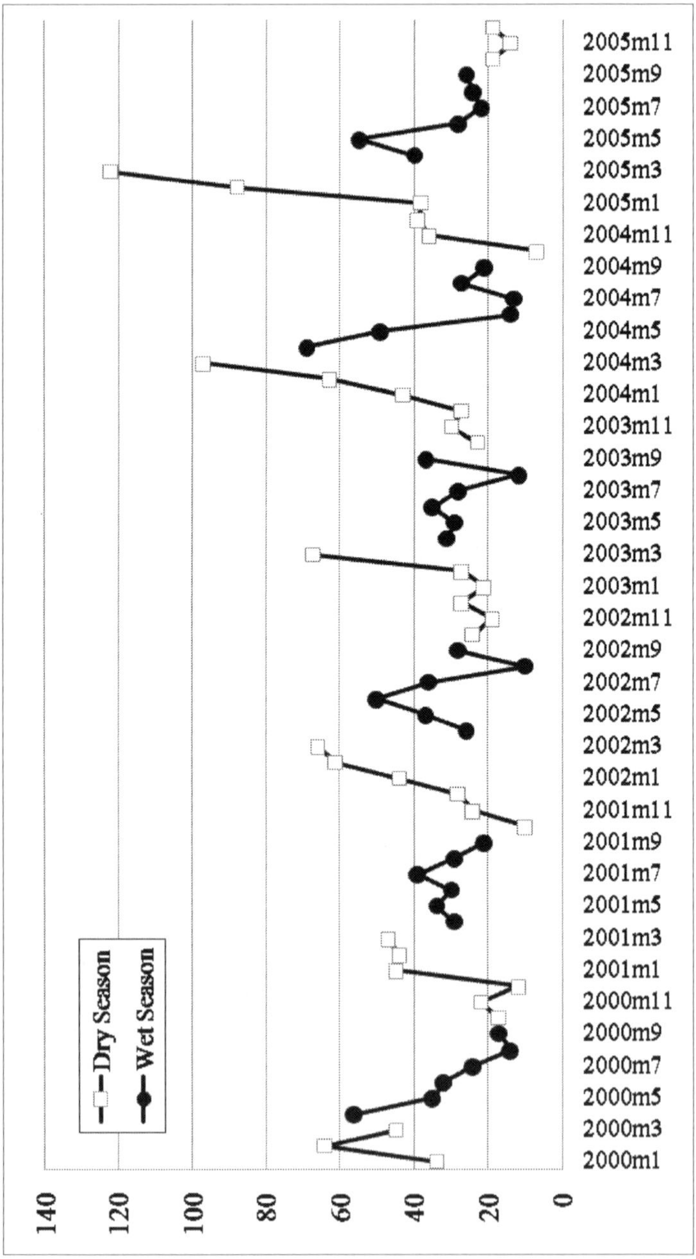

counts. The dry season starts in October and runs through March. The remaining months are considered wet-season months. Tampering incidents peak in March, the last dry-season month, and decline during the rainy-season months. Tampering occurs primarily during the dry season when food becomes scarcer and the soil has desiccated sufficiently to allow for the metal-search process to take place. Figure 5.3 compares March tampering statistics (the typical high month) to monthly averages, excluding March counts. When comparing March tampering counts to averages of the other months, observed increases range from 51.4% to 259.8%.

5.3. Supply Chain

The process of tampering may involve several exchanges, starting with the discovery and removal of landmines/UXO by an individual scrapper and ending with its final sale by a Cambodian border scrap yard master to a Thai or Vietnamese dealer. Following the discovery of ordnance, the individual scrapper may sell it either to a local scrap yard that temporarily houses the ordnance or to a middle-level transporter.

Middle-level transporters collect scrap either from individual scrappers or from local yards and deliver it to a final scrap yard located on the Thai or Vietnamese border. Once at the final scrap yard, yard masters sell it across international borders. Especially along the Vietnamese border, where ordnance is most commonly found, individual scrappers may skip the intermediate stages and sell ordnance directly to the final scrap yard master.

Next, I describe each phase in this supply chain, giving special attention to the search-perimeter exchange frequencies, travel methods, price markups, and decasing incentives.

5.3.1. Individual-level Scrapping

The scrap metal trade is an industry in Cambodia.[7] The process of initial tampering always begins with the discovery of a landmine or UXO, most often by individuals who actively search for scrap metal. The costs involved in searching for UXO scrap are considerably lower than those of searching for landmine scrap.

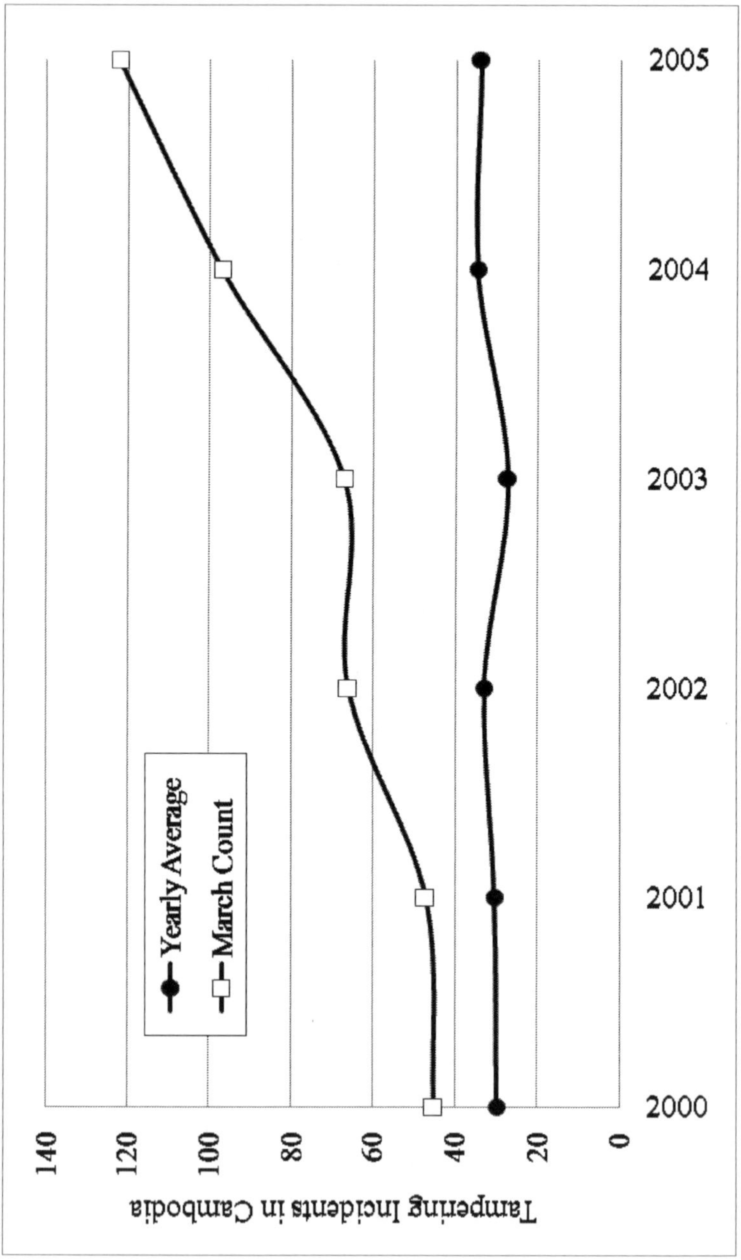

FIGURE 5.3. Comparison of Landmine/UXO Incidents Occurring in March to the Average Yearly Incident Count (2000–2005).

Due to this fact, scrapping behavior is more prevalent with UXO. However, tampering is not distinguished in this framework by ordnance type but rather by economic incentives. Metal scrapping in Cambodia involves both individuals who work for themselves and those affiliated with a group of scrappers. The vast majority of self-employed scrappers use a low-end metal detector, a digging device, and a collection bag. Prices of metal detectors, purchased in Vietnam, Thailand, or Phnom Penh, ranged between US$23 and $26 (in March 2008). Batteries used to operate metal detectors last anywhere between 40 and 100 hours of active use and cost between 4,000 and 5,500 riel (US$1.00–$1.38). Although this price appears to suggest ease of entry into the market, this amount of money is difficult to come by for Cambodia's most rural poor, leading to the establishment of loans to acquire metal-detecting devices. As an alternative to buying a metal detector, entrepreneurs are often eager to hire the labor of individual scrappers in exchange for a percentage of metal discovery.[8] Business owners typically replace batteries as part of the service they offer.

Scrappers frequently search in groups. The first advantage of searching in groups is that it facilitates recognizing, tracking, and recording areas that have been searched and economizes on time. Second, group search spreads the economic risk. As metal is discovered and sold daily, each member of the group receives an equivalent share of the income. Additionally, group search facilitates acquisition and information sharing regarding current prices and may even enable the negotiation of a better price. Finally, the search process often requires travel far from roads and locals. When individuals search for metal in a group, they secure a network of assistance in the event a landmine/UXO incident should occur.

Scrapping activities commence early in the morning and can last for the duration of the day. The typical individual-level scrapper searches within a radius of 1 to 2 kilometers per day. Individual-level scrappers travel on foot or cycle and often a combination of the two. Metal scrappers working for business owners often travel to a destination several kilometers from their local villages starting at 4:00 a.m. and lasting until the sun goes down.[9] Breaks are often taken for 2 to 3 hours in the middle of the day when the heat is unbearable.

Prospectors sell ordnance by weight to local scrap yard masters or middle transporters for cash. Local scrap yards serve as temporary holding centers and are spread throughout the countryside, with at least one per village. Individuals discovering metal make decisions about how frequently they carry ordnance to these sites based on the amount and weight of ordnance discovered, the distance to the local scrap yard, and their need for cash. If individuals live close to and are aware of middle-level transporters, they can avoid the local scrap yards altogether and gain a higher price for metal by trading directly with the middle-level transporter. On March 20, 2008, the price of metal received by individual-level scrappers was 800 riel/kilogram (US$0.20), a figure that appeared to be uniform throughout the country.[10] The law of "one price" holds due to arbitrage by the ubiquitous middle-level scrap transporters and the quick dissemination of price information.

The primary mover of the local price of metal is the price at the Thai border. Transporters continuously check the prices at the border by contacting the border yard masters via cellular telephones. Cell phones are operable in every district of Cambodia, assisting metal scrappers in establishing prices at every stage of the scrapping process.

Price adjustment disseminates from the top down. A lower border price reduces prices during the next rounds of transactions, which keeps the practice of markups relatively stable. A border price increase, however, does not trickle down as fast in an effort to raise markups. Price decreases are rare within the observable period of time since 1996.

Decasing ordnance is indisputably the most dangerous task in the process of tampering, and it may occur at any stage of the metal-scrapping process between the individual discovery and its sale across an international border. Ordnance can be decased in a variety of ways, all of which make ordnance casings indistinguishable from any other type of metal parcel. These methods include burning, lighting the fuses (when present), dropping from great heights, throwing against trees and rocks, prying with knives and sticks, and detonating with the use of explosives.[11]

Individual scrappers are subject to conflicting pressures regarding decasing. On the one hand, tampering is an illegal activity in Cambodia, punishable by fines, prison time, and often a combination of the two. Accordingly, individual-level scrappers sometimes attempt to avoid the fines and the possibility of internment by decasing ordnance before selling it. On the other hand, the majority of local scrap yards accept live ordnance, and decasing is therefore less likely to be attempted at the phase of individual discovery, following a risk transfer practice evident within tampering.

5.3.2. Local Scrap Yards and Middle-level Transporters

Individual scrappers usually sell ordnance directly to local scrap yards and sometimes to middle transporters. These local scrap yards bear the risk of housing ordnance in exchange for a monetary benefit. In March 2008, 800 riel/kilogram (US$0.20) was paid to the individual discovering the ordnance parcel. Local scrap yards simultaneously sold metal to middle-level transporters at 1,000 riel/kilogram (US$0.25).[12] Local scrap yards are necessary in establishing a reliable network within which ordnance and nonordnance metal can be sold. On average, one local scrap yard exists every 4 to 5 kilometers. Local scrap yards often open daily and pay cash to the individuals discovering metal immediately after weighing it.

Ordnance and nonordnance metal sits at local scrap yards awaiting the arrival of middle-level transporters. The majority of local scrap yards engage in transactions with middle-level transporters three or four times a week. Middle-level transporters deliver ordnance and nonordnance metal alike to final scrap yards on the Vietnam or Thailand borders.

Getting metal to the Thailand border may involve one individual carrying the metal the entire distance to the border towns or several individuals in turn. The methods of transportation are usually motorcycles, cars, and trucks. Often, metal transports are combined with the transport of other commercial goods, ferried up the Tonle Sap Lake, or joined with taxiing efforts between cities.

Metal traveling to the Vietnam border is most often delivered by the same transporter receiving it from a local scrap yard. The price of scrap metal for middle-transporters from final scrap yard masters on the Vietnam border was 1,120 riel/kilogram (US$0.28) in March 2008 and 2,600 riel/kilogram (US$0.65) on the Thai border. The difference in price is strong enough to induce some sellers discovering metal in provinces near the Cambodia–Vietnam border to transport it the nearly 560 kilometers from the east of the country to the final scrap yards near the Thailand border in spite of the apparent transportation costs.

Middle-level transporters that buy ordnance from local scrap yards not already decased also accept an increased risk of an incident occurring while transporting the ordnance. Often stored in a hot trunk or container, the metal and fuses can slowly warm to dangerous levels in the heat of the day. Additionally, vehicles constantly bump and bang down the poor-quality roads. This movement, especially combined with heated explosives, is a recipe for disaster. In spite of this risk, the majority of middle-level transporters opt to transport the ordnance intact and not undertake the risk of tampering.

5.3.3. Final Scrap Yards

Hundreds of final scrap yards exist near the Vietnam border, although, relative to those on the Cambodia–Thailand border, they are quite small. The yards near Vietnam are literally the backyards of the yard masters. The final scrap yards located near the Vietnam border receive scrap metal from middle-level transporters within a 12- to 14-kilometer radius. When middle-level transporters deliver metal to final scrap yards near the Cambodia–Vietnam border, a process of sorting and cleaning immediately commences. Metal parcels free of dirt and rust are sold for a higher price than those left dirty.

Final scrap yards near Vietnam were selling metal for an average price of 1,400 riel/kilogram (US$0.35) in March of 2008.[13] Vietnam sends large recovery trucks to collect from the final scrap yards on the Cambodian side of the border one to four times weekly.[14] Transportation costs incurred by the Vietnamese are no doubt reflected in the initial price of metal.

On the Cambodia–Thailand border are seven enormous final scrap yards.[15] Each of these yards houses thousands of tons of metal sorted into heaps that tower over the adjacent managerial buildings. Metal is funneled from the entire country toward these seven scrap yards. Massive sorting takes place following trade transactions between middle-level transporters and masters of each scrap yard. Ordnance is separated from other scrap and taken to a designated area. Ordnance cleared of explosives and those parcels still considered live are also separated. Ordnance casings that have already been hollowed out still require breaking and flattening before being considered nonordnance metal. In 1997, a landmine/UXO explosion took place at a final scrap yard in Cambodia, killing five Thai citizens. Following the massive press release that followed this incident, it became illegal to trade ordnance parcels with Thailand. In an effort to abide by these regulations and to avoid the penalties associated with breaking the rules, final scrap yards in Cambodia break apart ordnance casings to make them indistinguishable from any other parcels of scrap metal.

Landmines/UXO still considered live are sorted into another pile. In an effort to separate the metal casings from the explosives, yard masters contract out tampering work and require that the actual tampering take place away from the scrap yard. Often, people move from other parts of the country to take these jobs.[16] The frequency of tampering incidents occurring near the Cambodia–Thailand border indicates the extent of tampering taking place near the end of the metal-scrapping process. Metal at final scrap yards near the Thai border is weighed in large dual-trailer trucks on massive scales and sold to Thailand for an average price of 2,900 riel/kilogram (US$0.73).[17] Summary statistics for each of the stages of metal scrapping are reported in Table 5.1.

5.4. Metal Price Record

The price record consists of monthly data from March 1996 through April 2007 on various metals sold in final scrap yards in Poipet to Thai buyers. I compiled this information from the records of a scrap-yard broker who had been an accountant and who kept detailed notes on price quotes. Traded metals included hard and fragile metals, bronze and

TABLE 5.1. Cambodian Metal Scrapping Summary Statistics at Borders with Vietnam and Thailand.

	Cambodia-Vietnam Border Practices						
	Purchase Price*	Sell Price*	Markup %	Travel Distance	Transp. Method	Selling Frequency	Decasing Incentive
Individual Scrapper	n.a.	800/Kilo	n.a.	1 - 2 Km	Foot, cycle	Daily	Low
Home Scrap Yards	800 - 850/Kilo	1,000/Kilo	15-20%	4 - 5 Km	Foot, cycle	Daily	None
Mid-Level Transporters	1,000/Kilo	1,120/Kilo	12%	7-10 Km	Moto w/carts	3-4/Week	Low
Final Scrap Yards	1,120/Kilo	1,400/Kilo	25%	12-14 Km	Car, Truck, Moto	1-4/Week	High
	Cambodia-Thailand Border Practices						
	Purchase Price*	Sell Price*	Markup %	Travel Distance	Transp. Method	Selling Frequency	Decasing Incentive
Individual Scrapper	n.a.	800/Kilo	n.a.	1 - 2 Km	Foot, Cycle	Daily	Low
Home Scrap Yards	800 - 850/Kilo	1,000/Kilo	15-20%	4 - 5 Km	Foot, cycle	Daily	None
Mid-Level Transporters	1,000/Kilo	2,600/Kilo	225%	Across Country	Car, Truck, Moto	Weekly	Low
Final Scrap Yards	2,600/Kilo	2,900/Kilo	12%	n.a.	Truck	Weekly	High

Note. *Currency stated in Cambodian Riel. Stated prices as of March 20th, 2008. Exchange rate: 4,000 riel for $1.

brass, copper, lead, nonmagnetic,and ferrous metals. Additional communication with scrap brokers located along the border extended this record through December 2007. I converted price quotes, which were originally recorded at intervals as frequently as daily, to monthly averages.[18] Prices originally in the Thai currency (baht) are converted to Cambodian currency (riel).[19]

Over the 142-month span, prices for 41 months were missing. In order to obtain price information for the missing months, two additional data acquisition practices were employed.

The first method involved the comparison of metal scrap prices as they were sold to Thailand and the purchase price of rebar back from Thailand. Scrap metal sold to Thailand is often shipped to Bangkok and processed in smelting plants. Cambodia purchases metal back from Thailand in the form of rebar to be used in construction. Building owners often keep records of the prices of building supplies including rebar, from which information on missing scrap metal price can be gleaned.

In order to test whether a close relationship exists between the prices of scrap metal and rebar, I collected information on both prices from March to December 2008 (Meak, personal communications, March to December 2008).[20] The two prices are highly correlated. Furthermore, price comparisons indicate that the average difference between the two prices is 46.3%, ranging between 42.8% and 51.5%. Moving back in time, I was able to find rebar prices for 15 of the 41 missing months. I adjusted these prices by 46.3% and used them as scrap metal prices during the appropriate missing months.

Second, I compared the scrap price record with international metal price indices including world steel, world cold rolled steel, Chicago shredded scrap iron mill, Pittsburg shredded scrap iron mill, standard plate western European steel, USA steel, and China steel (Ustanis Klanois, 2009). Among these indices, the Thai border scrap metal price was most highly correlated (0.69) with the 2-month lagged world cold rolled metal price. Using percentage price changes of the lagged world cold rolled metal price, I interpolated the Thai border scrap metal price for the missing months. Figure 5.4 illustrates the relationship between rates of change of the two-period lagged world cold rolled metal and the border scrap metal price.

5.5. THE EMPIRICAL MODEL

In this section, I present four models to estimate the impact of scrap metal price on tampering. In addition to price, the model will also account for seasonal effects on tampering, bearing in mind the observed sharp increases in the dry season. The first two empirical models are:

$$\ln Y_t = \alpha + \beta \ln P_t + \delta M + \text{month dummies} + e_t \quad (5.1)$$

$$\ln Y_t = \alpha + \beta \ln P_t + \delta M + \text{month dummies} + \gamma_1 Y_{t-1} + \gamma_2 Y_{t-2} + e_t \quad (5.2)$$

where Y is the number of incidents across Cambodia, P is the price of scrap metal, M is the monthly trend to capture the secular trend, and e is the error term. T represents the monthly time index. In equation (5.2), one- and two-period lagged dependent variables are added to the right-hand side in view of the presence of serial correlation.

I also consider geographic variations in the relationship between scrap metal price and tampering. It may take longer for the Thai border price changes to disseminate to individual scrappers in the farther reaches of the country. Individuals traveling greater distances to sell ordnance on the Thai border also incur greater transportation costs. Thus, tampering in locations farther away from the border may be less responsive to price changes. Still, there are countervailing factors. First, as already mentioned, wide availability of cellular phones permits quick dissemination of information. Secondly, ordnance moves toward the border typically by "catching a ride" with other commerce and, therefore, transportation costs may be negligible.

Third, because eastern areas of Cambodia are more mountainous than central and western regions, precipitation drains into the lower areas in

FIGURE 5.4. Monthly Percent Change in the Price of World Cold-rolled Steel and the Cambodia-Thailand Border Record (May 2003–December 2007).

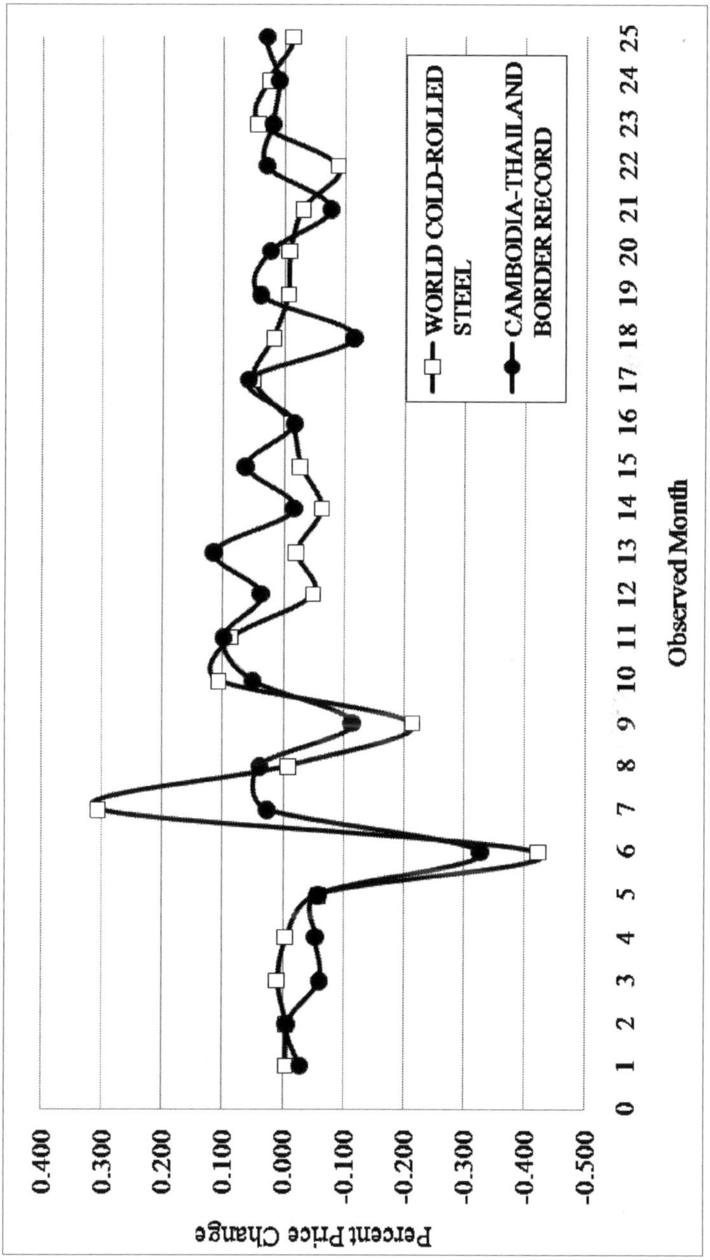

the bowl-shaped country. This makes tampering in the eastern regions more feasible during rainy-season months, suggesting higher responsiveness to price changes throughout the year.

In order to test for geographic variations, I identified three zones, distinguished in terms of the distance from the Thai border (Figure 5.5).[21] Zone 1 consists of provinces closest to the border. Zone 2 includes provinces more distant from the trading port, central in Cambodia's west–east geography. Last, Zone 3 involves provinces most distant from the Cambodia–Thailand border.[22]

In order to capture geographic variations in the price-tampering relationship, I measured the dependent variable as the monthly tampering incidents in each zone and pooled these observations. In addition to the price, trend, and monthly dummies of equation (5.1), I created additional explanatory variables of zone dummies, zone price, and zone month interactions.

The third empirical model is:

$$\begin{aligned}\ln Y_{zt} = \alpha + \beta \ln P_t + \delta M &+ \text{zone dummies} \\ &+ \text{month dummies} + \text{zone and price interaction} \\ &+ \text{zone and month interaction} + e_{zt}\end{aligned} \tag{5.3}$$

where z is an index for geographic zone.

None of these models incorporates the insights of the previous chapters, which emphasized economic need as a determinant of tampering activity. Due the lack of data, while testing this hypothesis in the time series context, it is not feasible to test for the price effect controlling for economic need or the availability of agricultural products. As a first approximation, however, I use agricultural year fixed effects to control for year-to-year variations in agricultural production from 1996 to 2007. Each agricultural season runs from April, the beginning of the rainy season, to March at the end of the dry-season. The fourth empirical model is:

$$\ln Y_t = \alpha + \beta \ln P_t + \delta M + \text{month dummies} + \text{year dummies} + e_t \tag{5.4}$$

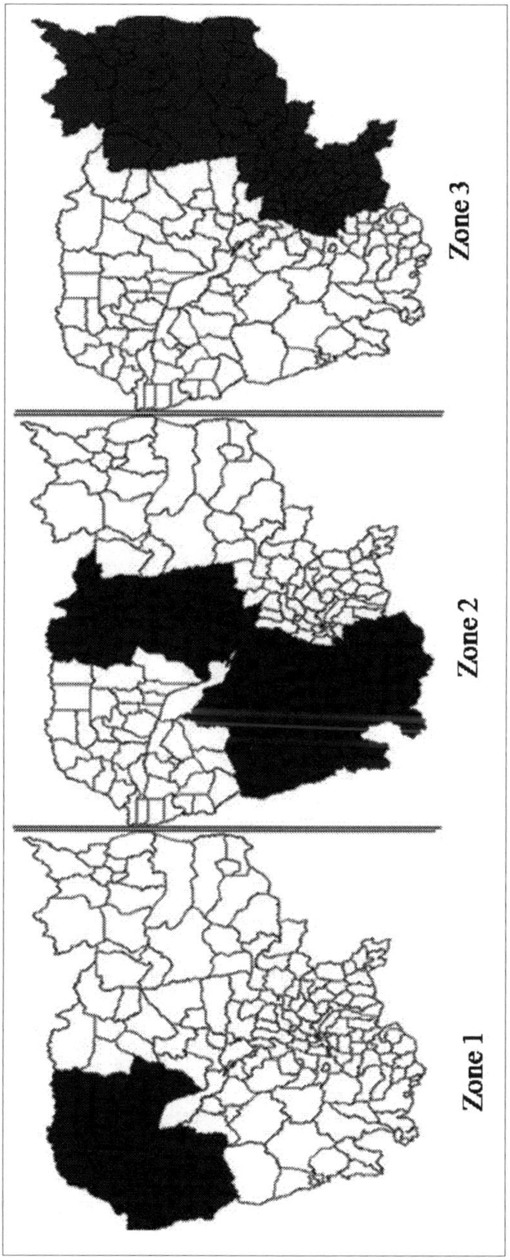

Figure 5.5. Geographic Zone Distinctions Used to Test Tampering Responsiveness to Price Fluctuations at the Cambodia-Thailand Border.

5.6. Estimation Results

5.6.1. Models 5.1 and 5.2

The estimates of equation 5.1 are displayed in Table 5.2. In this first model, I used accidents in addition to tampering as a dependent variable for purposes of comparison. The first two columns of the table report the findings for accidents and the last two for tampering. Second, in order to check the sensitivity of the estimates in regard to the missing 41 observations, I also ran separate regressions that excluded these observations. Thus, each regression is run separately with 100 and 141 observations.

According to Table 5.2, 80% to 90% of the variation in accidents and close to 60% in tampering is explained by the explanatory variables. Results are also consistent across the original and adjusted datasets and are, therefore, quite robust. Both accidents and tampering declined secularly over time.

More precisely, this finding indicates that for every 1% increase in the price of metal, tampering will experience a subsequent increase of 1.4%. and is very high regarding statistical significance, indicating a strong link between the two variables. This finding provides evidence supporting the hypothesis that scrappers respond to price stimuli.

While accidents prove less significant in magnitude and statistical significance, it is surprising that accidents prove a positive relationship with the price of scrap metal. One possible explanation is that an individual's engagement in metal search results in landmine-related accidents. If this is the case, then perhaps it would be more accurate to classify accidents that take place during prospecting as tampering. The strict definition of tampering I used may have led to the undercounting of landmine/UXO tampering incidents.

As is illustrated in Table 5.3, landmine/UXO accidents are higher in the month of March ($p < 0.10$), and lower in September to December ($p < 0.01$). March is the end of the dry season, which means farmers engage in traditional buffalo-driven tilling practices to prepare the soil for planting. People are also more vulnerable to hunger in March, which is at the end of the harvest cycle. The flood status of rice fields during

TABLE 5.2. Impact of the Price of Metal on Landmine/UXO Incidents (Model 5.1).

	Accidents		Tampering	
	Original Price Record	Adjusted Price Record	Original Price Record	Adjusted Price Record
Price	0.46	0.41	1.48	1.35
	(0.22)**	(0.18)**	(0.30)***	(0.23)***
February	0.2	0.08	0.45	0.21
	-0.18	-0.14	(0.24)**	-0.18
March	0.42	0.22	0.59	0.39
	(0.17)***	(0.14)*	(0.23)***	(0.18)**
April	0.13	0.08	0.15	0.02
	-0.17	-0.14	-0.24	-0.18
May	0.21	0.02	0.24	0.11
	-0.17	-0.14	-0.23	-0.18
June	0.11	-0.07	0.16	-0.04
	-0.16	-0.14	-0.23	-0.18
July	0.14	-0.07	0.14	-0.22
	-0.18	-0.14	-0.25	-0.18
August	0.23	-0.09	-0.15	-0.35
	-0.17	-0.14	-0.24	(0.18)**
September	-0.23	-0.46	-0.29	-0.39
	(0.17)*	(0.14)***	-0.23	(0.18)**
October	-0.27	-0.42	-0.45	-0.62
	(0.17)*	(0.14)***	(0.23)**	(0.18)***
November	-0.22	-0.17	-0.39	-0.36
	-0.18	-0.14	(0.24)*	-0.18
December	-0.1	-0.34	0.13	-0.06
	-0.16	(0.14)***	-0.23	-0.18
Monthly trend	-0.02	-0.02	-0.01	-0.01
	(0.001)***	(0.001)***	(0.002)***	(0.001)***
Constant	3.1	3.42	-1.65	-1.08
	-0.78	-0.66	-1.08	-0.84
N	100	141	100	141
R-squared	0.88	0.833	0.574	0.551
Adj R-squared	0.862	0.816	0.51	0.505
F Stat	48.4	48.8	8.92	12
Prob. > F	0	0	0	0
Durbin-Watson	1.176	1.474	1.121	1.333

Note. Standard errors in parenthesis. *Significant at the 10 percent level, **Significant at the 5 percent level, ***Significant at 1 percent.

TABLE 5.3. Impact of the Price of Metal on Tampering (Model 5.2).

	Model 5.1	Model 5.2a	Model 5.2b
Price	1.35 (0.23)***	1.21 (0.23)***	1.21 (0.23)***
February	0.21 -0.18	0.19 -0.18	0.18 -0.18
March	0.39 (0.18)**	0.31 (0.18)*	0.3 (0.18)*
April	0.02 -0.18	-0.05 -0.18	-0.07 -0.19
May	0.11 -0.18	0.06 -0.17	0.05 -0.19
June	-0.04 -0.18	-0.09 -0.17	-0.12 -0.18
July	-0.22 -0.18	-0.23 -0.18	-0.27 (0.18)*
August	-0.35 (0.18)**	-0.32 (0.18)**	-0.35 (0.18)**
September	-0.39 (0.18)**	-0.34 (0.18)**	-0.36 (0.18)**
October	-0.62 (0.18)***	-0.57 (0.18)***	-0.57 (0.18)***
November	-0.36 -0.18	-0.23 -0.18	-0.24 -0.18
December	-0.06 -0.18	-0.01 -0.17	0.02 -0.18
Monthly trend	-0.01 (0.001)***	-0.01 (0.001)***	-0.01 (0.001)***
Tampering Lag 1		0.19 (0.08)***	0.16 (0.08)**
Tampering Lag 2			0.08 -0.08
Constant	-1.08 -0.84	-1.25 -0.82	-1.34 -0.83
N	141	140	139
R-squared	0.551	0.583	0.591
Adj R-squared	0.505	0.536	0.541
F	12	12.48	11.85
Prob.>F	0	0	0
Durbin's h	1.333	1.825	1.794

Note. Standard errors in parenthesis. *Significant at the 10 percent level, **Significant at the 5 percent level, ***Significant at the 1 percent level.

the last few months of the year prevents landmine/UXO accidents from taking place as frequently as in other months. Tampering incidents also reflect strong wet- and dry-season associations. Tampering rises in the month of March ($p < 0.05$), increasing on average by 39%. During August, September, and October, tampering is less frequent and not as statistically significant. The Durbin-Watson statistics, however, indicate there is a higher degree of autocorrelation in the error term. While this does not bias the OLS coefficients, positive autocorrelation underestimates the standard errors.

Figure 5.2 suggests monthly tampering incidents are serially correlated. Therefore, Model 5.2 introduces lagged dependent variables into the model. The first column of Table 5.3 reproduces tampering results from Table 5.2 with the adjusted price record. The remaining two columns add one- and two-period lagged tampering to the right-hand side.

Regardless of the specification, Table 5.2 shows that scrap metal price is an important variable in explaining tampering. The estimated elasticity drops slightly, from 1.35 to 1.21, but is still statistically significant at the 1% level. The coefficients of month dummies are also similar, although the value for the March coefficient declines by about a quarter and is now only statistically significant at the 10% level.

It is also noteworthy that Durbin's h-statistic now suggests no autocorrelation of the error term, which attests to the robustness of t-statistics.

5.6.2. Zone Model

Estimates of Model 5.3 are reported in Table 5.4. The first column lists the estimates for Zone 1, which is composed of provinces geographically closest to the main Cambodia–Thailand metal trading port in Poipet. The response of tampering to price changes in this zone is nearly proportionate; suggesting that a 1% increase in price leads to a near 1% increase in tampering. The second and third column report estimates of Zone 2 and Zone 3 dummies, respectively. The price elasticities in the respective zones equal 0.67 (1.07–0.40) and 1.89 (1.07+0.82). While all elasticities are positive, important geographic differences exist. Zone 1, referencing the areas within Cambodia nearest the Thai border, incurs the greatest

TABLE 5.4. Impact of the Price of Metal on Tampering (Model 5.3).

	Zone 1	Zone 2	Zone 3
Price	1.07	-0.4	0.82
	(0.29)***	-0.3	(0.30)***
February	0.21	0.15	-0.08
	-0.31	-0.44	-0.44
March	0.49	-0.39	0.29
	(0.32)*	-0.45	-0.45
April	-0.09	0.25	0.3
	-0.31	-0.44	-0.44
May	0.16	-0.29	0.19
	-0.31	-0.44	-0.44
June	-0.24	0.2	0.54
	-0.31	-0.44	-0.44
July	-0.45	0.07	0.52
	(0.31)*	-0.44	-0.44
August	-0.34	-0.42	0.27
	-0.31	-0.44	-0.44
September	-0.82	0.12	1.01
	(0.31)***	-0.44	(0.44)***
October	-0.88	0.01	0.66
	(0.31)***	-0.44	-0.44
November	-0.79	0.76	0.45
	(0.31)***	-0.44	-0.44
December	-0.11	0.12	-0.14
	-0.31	-0.44	-0.44
Monthly trend	-0.01		
	(0.001)***		
Constant	-0.76	1	-4.55
	1.1	1.23	1.23***
Observations	423		
R-squared	0.464		
Adj R-squared	0.41		
F	8.51		
Prob. > F	0		

Note. Standard errors in parenthesis. *Significant at the 10 percent level, **Significant at the 5 percent level, ***Significant at the 1 percent level.

number of absolute and relative tampering incidents. Additionally, as the regression indicates, for every 1% increase in the price of metal in this zone, tampering incidents increase by 1.07%. This finding is statistically significant at the 1% level. For the same 1% increase in the price of metal, tampering in Zone 3 increases by 1.89%, indicating a strong elastic response. This finding is also statistically significant at the 1% level.

Tampering response to the price of metal in Zone 2 is not correlated to a statistically significant degree. It is likely that regions falling within this zone are not price responsive because no market for metal exists within this zone.

Additionally, the existence of ordnance (mostly UXO) primarily falls to the east of this zone's boundaries. While a certain number of tampering incidents will occur where ordinance is initially discovered or where it is eventually decased (primarily in Zone 1), it is likely that ordnance is simply passing through Zone 2. In fact, it is critical to point out that despite the fact that the elasticity response to the price of metal is stronger in Zone 3 than in Zone 1, more tampering incidents are occurring in Zone 1. The estimated relationships between scrap metal price and zone tampering are illustrated in Figure 5.6. This finding provides evidence that the bulk of the risk inherent in the tampering process is taking place after ordnance is found and transported near the Cambodia–Thailand border. Additionally, this finding verifies that in spite of cost increases incurred while transporting the ordnance toward the western border, realized profits are greater when trading with the western neighbor.

It has, therefore, been substantiated that as the price of metal climbs, those experiencing poverty, economic need, or agricultural vulnerability respond to the price incentives by engaging in tampering. This tampering behavior is initiated and very price responsive in the areas most heavily inundated with ordnance (Zone 3), but reflected in greatest magnitude where the bulk of incidents are occurring (Zone 1).

In regard to observations made regarding zones and months, the notable observation is in regard to tampering increases evident during the month of September in Zone 3. While previous month effects concentrated on March subsequent to agricultural realities experienced at the end of the dry season, zone effects capture a statistically significant finding for September within the third zone. It is likely this result is the outcome of distinct geographic conditions experienced in Zone 3.

More specifically, September falls at the end of the rainy season in Cambodia. While this reality is the same for all three distinguished zones, the altitude in Zone 3 is, on average, much greater than for the other two zones. Additionally, the western and central regions of Cambodia (Zones 1 and 2) contain the Tonle Sap Lake, a massive contracting and expanding body of water. Zones containing the Tonle Sap are lower in altitude and are more likely to have flooded fields and plains. Higher altitudes in Zone 3, in conjunction with the bowl-like geography of Cambodia's landscape, produce land more conducive to tampering activities. Accordingly, while vulnerabilities may be experienced unilaterally throughout the country during this month, tampering options are greater in Zone 3 due to geographic idiosyncrasies.

5.6.3. Year Fixed Effects

Estimates of model 5.4 are presented in Table 5.5. None of the findings reported earlier concerning price elasticity, monthly trend, or month fixed effects are altered by including year effects. One interesting result is that tampering increased in 1998, 1999, and 2004 ($p < 0.01$ in each). Each of these years experienced a dramatic reduction (10% or greater) in net rice yields in at least one of the districts in Cambodia. Similar to the findings in Chapter 4, therefore, it appears tampering is related to agricultural vulnerability. It is critical, therefore, for policy makers to track agricultural output levels and associate low levels of production with increased incentives to tamper with ordnance.

5.7. Policy Recommendations

The majority of landmine/UXO incidents in Cambodia since 1999 have been due to tampering. Reported estimations in this chapter presented evidence for the first time supporting the hypothesis that the price of scrap metal affects tampering directly. From a social policy perspective, this implies that efforts to reduce tampering incidents should take into account market forces—specifically, scrap metal prices. Toward this end, I suggest two policy interventions: the simultaneous implementation of scrap metal price controls at the Cambodia–Thailand border and on-site cash payment programs for ordnance at the point of discovery. Section 5.6.1 will consider the implications of metal price controls and Section 5.6.2 will discuss the ramifications of implementing on-site ordnance payment programs.

5.7.1. Metal Price Controls

The establishment of price controls at the Cambodia–Thailand border has long been suggested by both government and nongovernmental organizations as a measure to combat tampering (McGrath, 1994). In spite of these suggestions, price controls have primarily not been implemented due to the lack of evidence linking tampering to the price of metal. Supporting evidence now exists.

In addition to a dearth of data linking tampering behavior to the price of metal, price fixing is controversial from an economic perspective due to the existence of a dead-weight loss that occurs when price ceilings are implemented. More precisely, price fixing limits the price sellers can obtain when engaging in trade. The decrease in price reduces incentives to remain active within the market. Both consumer surplus and producer surplus would be decreased, thus limiting the amount of value created within the scrap trade. Accordingly, if Cambodia imposed a price ceiling on metal in accordance with the established (and lower) price on the Cambodia–Vietnam border, incentives to tamper would be drastically reduced, but this would come at a cost. In addition to a decreased total surplus experienced within the market for metal, this would also create an excess demand for metal in Thailand.

An excess demand for metal in Thailand would increase import demands from other surrounding countries also suffering from landmine/UXO contamination (specifically Laos and Myanmar). Price fixing could, therefore, result in a chain of unintended and undesirable consequences.

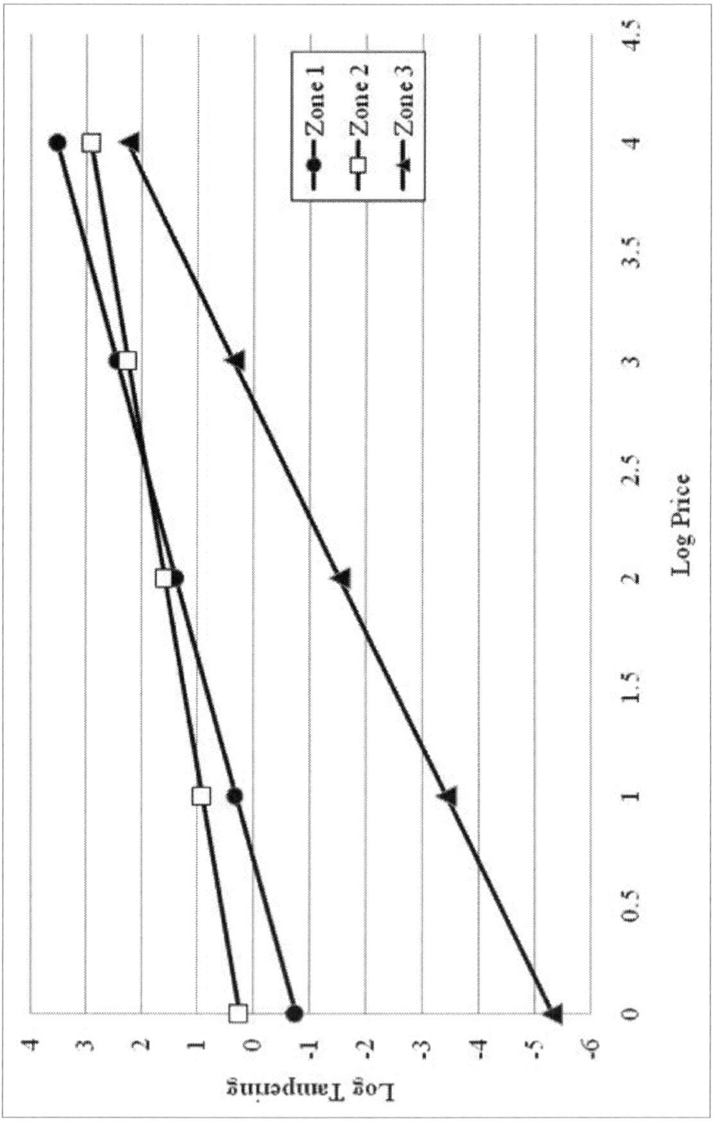

FIGURE 5.6. Zone-Specific Tampering Elasticities in Cambodia.

Table 5.5. Year-specific Landmine/UXO Tampering and the Price of Metal Regression Estimates.

	Coefficient	Std. Err.
Price	1.86	0.31***
February	0.18	0.16
March	0.35	0.16**
April	0.02	0.16
May	0.16	0.16
June	0.02	0.16
July	-0.13	0.16
August	-0.27	0.16*
September	-0.3	0.16**
October	-0.51	0.17***
November	-0.3	0.16**
December	0	0.16
Month Count	-0.01	0.002***
1997	-0.16	0.15
1998	0.54	0.14***
1999	0.33	0.14***
2000	0.01	0.14
2001	-0.02	0.15
2002	-0.23	0.16*
2003	0.05	0.17
2004	0.47	0.15***
2005	0.21	0.16
2006	0.22	0.16*
Constant	-2.96	1.1
Number of Observations	141	
R-squared	0.68	
Adj R-squared	0.617	
Root MSE	0.374	
F	10.79	
Prob. > F	0	

Note. *Significant at the 10 percent level, **Significant at the 5 percent level, ***Significant at the 1 percent level.

Any consideration of price fixing should accordingly be established in coordination with the other countries with conditions similar to Cambodia in order to avoid simply transferring the burden from one country to another.

Price controls could also complicate trade relations between Cambodia and Thailand. Specifically, the imposition of metal-trade restrictions may complicate relations of international trade between these two countries. Organizations arguing in favor of pricing instruments should actively engage trade sanction members in an effort to minimize the negative implications that could follow.

More importantly, individuals in the most vulnerable situations are forced into scrapping and tampering behavior. With the implementation of price fixing, metal scrapping becomes an activity with a significant decrease in monetary compensation, which may force those in the most vulnerable of situations to scrap and tamper more by engaging in trade within the black market. These effects are not desirable. It is entirely possible, therefore, that instituting price controls could have the reverse of the effect intended by critically impairing the population it was designed to help. Implementing price controls alone, therefore, will not prove effective. Implementing price controls in tandem with on-site payment programs, however, can provide the desired solution.

5.7.2. On-site Ordnance Payment Programs

The control of prices would not prove sufficient in decreasing tampering because of the likely emergence of a black market. A more radical policy approach could include on-site ordnance payment programs in addition to border price controls. Information could quickly disseminate though channels of mine-risk education, informing Cambodians that when they discover landmine-related ordnance, the landmine community will reimburse them for the weight of the ordnance. Immediately upon discovering the ordnance, Cambodians will be instructed to contact the nearest landmine affiliate operating in Cambodia, either directly or by means of their village leaders. The landmine affiliate will then travel to the ordnance location, safely disarm or remove the ordnance parcel, and reimburse the discovering party.

By enforcing both price fixing and on-site ordnance payment programs, policy makers could transfer the risk of tampering from the hands of the untrained to those skilled in ordnance disposal techniques.

The low price of metal at the border in conjunction with cash payments for metal by the landmine community would dissuade Cambodians from personally taking on the risk of tampering. While at the same time providing incentives to discover landmine-related ordnance, there would be no reason for individuals to take upon themselves the risk of tampering when landmine affiliates have guaranteed the same compensation rates without the absorption of risk. Price controls instituted in conjunction with on-site payment programs would dramatically reduce the risks scrappers face without having adverse effects on their livelihood.

Benefits coming from this policy enactment must be considered in conjunction with the costs associated with the implementation of the policy. The direct costs of initiating an on-site payment program while at the same time controlling the price of metal at the border can likely be afforded by transferring a portion of mine-risk education funding dollars toward the program. While outside the scope of this book, the cost-benefit analysis of this policy should be performed.

ENDNOTES

1. As was established in Chapter 2, the proportion of tampering incidents after 1999 has been greater than those resulting from agriculture- and travel-related incidents.
2. The Royal Government of Cambodia, Cambodian Mine Action Authority, and Cambodian Mine Action Center have all suggested that this relationship exists.
3. In Richard Moyes' "Tampering" report, he finds that more than 50% of men and boys in high-risk communities had handled or destroyed ordnance.
4. Metal is not sold to the third neighbor, Laos. Laos suffered a fate similar to Cambodia's and also sells postwar scrap to Thailand and Vietnam.
5. Cambodia is in the process of acquiring the technology to recast metal.
6. The process of discovering UXO is not as dangerous as the discovery of a landmine. Landmines are designed to detonate during the discovery process, whereas UXO failed to detonate when dropped from war planes.
7. This is similar to a statement made by Richard Moyes concerning Laos (Moyes, 2005).
8. Several metal scrappers in the Svay Rieng province indicated that they pay between 10% and 20% of their findings to business owners. Metal was most often exchanged with middle-level transporters through channels established by the business owner in order to minimize pilfering.
9. Business owners will sometimes provide transportation to locations known to yield large amounts of metal.
10. Comparisons were made in the Svay Rieng and Krong Pailin provinces to verify that individuals were receiving the same monetary remuneration at the eastern and western extremes of the country.
11. Methods listed were mentioned by various individuals across Cambodia while researching in February 2007, April 2007, and March 2008. Burning ordnance and lighting the fuses were the most common methods.
12. Price information personally collected during March 2008 research trip.
13. Dirty metal was selling for 1,250 riel/kilogram, only a slight markup from the price paid to the middle-level transporter. Clean metal was selling for as high as 1,600 riel/kilogram. Only a small portion of dirty metal was deemed suitable to clean. The majority of dirty metal was sold in the same condition that in which it was purchased.
14. The frequency of metal pickups depends on Vietnam's demand for metal, the speed at which final scrap yards receive metal, and weather conditions.

15. Almost all metal traded with Thailand is transferred through the border town known as Poipet. In accordance with trade agreements between the two countries, final scrap yards in this town are the only locations legally allowed to trade with Thailand.
16. Military personnel often feel that wartime experience uniquely qualifies them to handle landmines/UXO. As mentioned in Chapter 3, sex ratios in districts near the Cambodia–Thailand border are in favor of men.
17. Due to the magnitude of metal traded, clean and dirty distinctions are not nearly as important on the Thai border.
18. The frequency of price records varies from between 1 and 29 observations monthly.
19. Baht is the currency used in Thailand and in many places in Cambodia near the Cambodia–Thailand border. The record was kept in baht because the scrap broker to whom the record belongs was from Thailand.
20. The assistance of Somnang Meak facilitated the acquisition of price data between March and December of 2007.
21. Zone boundaries were composed with the distance from the Poipet trading port in mind. In accordance with the major roadways on both sides of the Tonle Sap, I calculated the distance from Poipet to the center of each district.
22. Zone 1: Banteay Mean Chey, Battambang, Krong Pailin, Otdar Mean Chey, and Siem Reap provinces. Zone 2: Kampong Chhnang, Kampong Speu, Kampong Thom, Kampot, Kaoh Kong, Krong Kaeb, Krong Preah Sihanouk, Phnom Penh, Preah Vihear, Pursat and Takeav. Zone 3: Kampong Cham, Kandal, Kracheh, Mondol Kiri, Prey Veaeng, Rotanak Kir, Stueng Traeng, and Svay Rieng.

Chapter 6

Conclusion

Cambodia is the only country in the world with more active landmines than people.[1] These landmines were laid over time by various warring factions, including Royal Government Forces, Khmer Rouge, Thailand border protectionists, and the Vietnamese-backed People's Republic of Kampuchea. US carpet bombing raids dropped 540,000 tons of bombs on Cambodia. A significant portion of this ordnance is still live and continues to litter the countryside. The combination of landmines and UXO in Cambodia in conjunction with human action (both accidental and tampering related) resulted in 58,000 incidents between 1980 and 2007.

In response to the landmine/UXO problem in Cambodia, a formal demining sector was established in 1992 with five adopted pillars of mine action. According to these pillars, mine-action priorities are landmine removal, mine-risk education, explosive ordnance disposal, victim assistance, and stockpile destruction.

These efforts, however, ignore the impact of social and economic factors on landmine/UXO incidents. This book first made a distinction between accidents and tampering incidents. Because tampering involves intentional handling of ordnance, the factors underlying these two types of incidents are expected to be distinct. This book then statistically explored the effect of socioeconomic conditions, reflecting the impact of economic vulnerability on each incident type. These links are expected to assist policy makers in their attempts to reduce the occurrence of mine-related incidents.

The first hypothesis is that the frequency of landmine/UXO incidents is influenced by economic need. For this purpose, I identified several variables at the district level symptomatic of poverty and economic need. I have also included control variables in the analysis: age dependence, single-parent dependence, formal education measurements, energy sources used for cooking, access to safe drinking water, rural–urban status, K5 districts, migration, population density, and sex ratio. I performed regressions on these variables for the accident, tampering, and pooled incidents between 1996 and 2000 for a cross section of 185 districts, paying special attention to the spatial effects that might confound estimation.

Estimates show that socioeconomic factors are important in predicting the frequency of incidents, and there are differences between the determinants of accidents and tampering incidents. Accidents rise with higher single-parent dependency, migration, male/female sex ratio, and K5 district locations. Tampering, by contrast, is directly affected by higher single-parent dependency, firewood cooking dependency (signaling poverty), population density, sex ratio, lower rates of education, and K5 district associations.

Policy makers should take note of the relationship between poverty, economic need, and landmine/UXO incidents. Current mine-action approaches can be improved by noting the relationship between the various socioeconomic measures and landmine/UXO accidents and tampering. Furthermore, policy makers should track various measures of poverty and economic need, understanding that as these conditions worsen, individuals will engage in more risky activities and likely incur a greater incident rate within both accident and tampering classifications.

The second contribution of the book shows that agricultural factors influence landmine/UXO incidents. I used a panel of 26 provinces over the 1998 to 2006 agricultural periods to estimate how pooled landmine/UXO incidents, as well as accidents and tampering individually, are affected by agricultural conditions. Accidents rise as water supplies, rice yields, and crop diversification decrease. Tampering incidents rise when there is a decrease in net rice per capita, water supplies, rice yields, crop diversification, and nonrice yields per capita. Tampering incidents also rise when there is an increase in droughts and floods. I suggest policy makers utilize this information in an effort to reduce landmine/UXO incidents by creating a sustainable irrigation-based infrastructure, implementing high-yield rice varieties, providing initial seed-stock supplies, and diversifying crops.

The third contribution of this book is the estimation of the elasticity of tampering with respect to the price of scrap metal. Tampering has been the source of most of the landmine/UXO incidents since 1999. The rise in tampering incidents can be traced back to the increased Thai demand for scrap metal from Cambodia following rapid economic growth in China, which reduced Chinese metal exports. I compiled monthly price series for Thai border scrap metal from April 1996 to December 2007 to test the hypothesis that tampering responds to price signals. In the absence of such a dataset, this hypothesis has never before been tested. Estimates show tampering is more than unitary price elastic (around 1.4). In addition, there are substantial differences between specific zones throughout the country. I suggest metal price-fixing instruments be implemented in conjunction with on-site ordnance payment programs. These actions would assist in demining Cambodia without exposing untrained individuals to the risk involved in decasing ordnance.

Mine-action organizations in Cambodia have made significant efforts to reduce the impact of landmine/UXO contamination on people by engaging in efforts of demining, mine-risk education, and victim assistance. Despite these efforts, individuals in situations of poverty and economic need continue to risk their lives inadvertently or intentionally in an effort to feed themselves and their families. While demining and mine-risk education initiatives will undoubtedly remain prerogatives of the mine-action community, particular attention should also be given to decreasing the number of incidents taking place by targeting the socioeconomic, agricultural, and price-related factors shown to have critical ramifications. Finally, policy makers should reconstruct their approaches in a way that recognizes tampering incidents comprise the majority of incidents. Addressing poverty and economic need will ultimately reduce the occurrence of both landmine accidents and tampering.

Moving Forward

Poverty and economic need are clearly and unequivocally linked to landmine/UXO incidents in Cambodia. This reality takes specific shape in regard to both accidents and tampering. This report has emphasized the fact that the majority of incidents in Cambodia are now due to tampering. Notwithstanding this fact, accident and tampering rates have both been individually connected with various agricultural, socioeconomic, and economic factors. This information can be informative to policy makers. While I have made policy suggestions, it is likely these suggestions can be significantly improved upon. Each policy measure must be subjected to rigorous cost-benefit analysis. Additionally, it is likely myriad alternative policy prescriptions will be suggested by Mine Action practitioners. In addition to continued study that should take place in regard to using these findings in ordnance amelioration efforts, close attention must be paid to the variables that help to predict changing landmine/UXO incidents. While the information discovered in this effort is interesting and informative, it is useless without practical application. Any effort to reduce the impact of ordnance in Cambodia must first understand the interconnected relations existing between landmine/UXO incidents, poverty, and economic need. All that remains is a concerted effort to use this information in a way that will accomplish the desired result. While much work remains to be done in implementing these findings appropriately, many critical relationships have been identified. If we are truly concerned about reducing the impact ordnance has on people, it is paramount to remember that people respond to incentives. Landmine/UXO accidents and tampering incidents have been shown to follow situations of economic need and poverty. As people become economically vulnerable, they seek ways to avoid the pains of hunger and ameliorate penury. Oftentimes, this means taking on activities involving a substantial amount of risk. While eventual efforts to remove landmine-related ordnance from Cambodia's soil may one day prove successful, it is critical to focus the majority of efforts at the present time on preventing incidents from occurring. By targeting factors of poverty and economic need, this goal can be successfully accomplished.

ENDNOTE

1. Landmine Monitor keeps information about landmines throughout the world. Currently, 82 countries suffer a residual landmine/UXO problem. The magnitude of ordnance varies among countries and states. Estimates concerning the number of landmine-related parcels in each country place Cambodia at the top of the list in relation to population statistics. Specifically, landmine-to-population ratios in Cambodia are at 1.53. Countries that come closest in comparison are Bosnia and Herzegovina with a ratio of .78, Croatia at .67, Angola at .57, Iraq at .36, Egypt at .29, Iran at .24, and Rwanda at .03. In addition to landmine counts, the existence of UXO dramatically increases the magnitude of residual ordnance parcels.

Appendix A

Narratives From the Field

A.1. US Carpet Bombers

S. P. was born in July of 1952 to her parents P. and R.[1] At the time of her birth, S. P.'s family was living in the Tboung Khmum district in the Kampong Cham province. S. P. was the fifth of seven children. S. P. remembers growing up in Cambodia as a happy, carefree child. At the age of 9, S. P. contributed to the New Year celebration by collecting stunning arrangements of flowers for the floating parade. She gathered pink and white orchids mixed with long-stemmed yellow and lavender lotus flowers and placed them in various bouquets and garlands. S. P. delivered the assortment of flowers to her mother's sister the morning of the celebration. She ran barefoot down a well-traveled dusty path that eventually led to the river. She smiled when she caught sight of her eldest brother M. high in the treetops. M. had secured her a luxurious view of the upcoming parade in a majestic banyan tree hanging a considerable distance over the river. As the parade passed beneath the shade tree, she enthusiastically detected each handcrafted arrangement scattered among the continual chain of vessels. Each passing craft symbolized the unique recognition of abundance Cambodians enjoyed. As the traditional songs of New Year reached diminuendo in the distance, she followed M. into the river by jumping from the high branches of their friendly tree.

Following S. P.'s 12th birthday, she took journey with her brothers R. and N. to stay with their cousins in the Stueng Traeng province for a few weeks. Shabby, unpaved roads mixed with an abundance of hard-falling rain eventually forced their transportation into a deeply trenched mud pool. A unanimous decision was made by the siblings to continue their journey on foot. As S. P., R., and N. strolled toward their destination, they frequently crossed rice-paddy fields. R. was captivated by the abundance of crabs and the expeditious escape paths established by each crustacean. As the three siblings focused their labors within a sufficiently diminutive area, they quickly learned advantageous techniques for catching the elusive tamarind crabs. A sufficient amount of sumptuous crabmeat provided relief from hunger the duration of their journey.

S. P. was supposed to be married at the age of 14 to U. V., a 28-year-old friend of the family. Reluctant to enter into a forced marriage, S. P. coerced M. into taking her with him on work-related delivery of food to the Kaev Seima district in the Mondol Kiri province. Throughout the journey, she discussed the possibility of moving in with a friend in a distant province to avoid the undesired and compulsory union. M. offered support to S. P. in spite of the bride price compensation that would be afforded their parents during this time of extreme economic hardship. M. agreed to assist S. P. in collecting her limited belongings in the Tboung Khmum district before making the clandestine journey to her hideaway.

As S. P. and M. approached their hometown, M. noticed an overturned company vehicle an abnormal distance from the accustomed path of travel. M. stopped his vehicle as near as possible to the overturned vehicle and darted toward the incident. As charged by M., S. P. remained in the vehicle as a powerless onlooker. Immediately after M. reached the upended vehicle, a body was pulled free and dangled across M.'s flexed arms in an effort to return to seek help. An innate proclivity compelled S. P. to assist M. in his efforts. As she stepped away from the discernible path, a deafening screech filled the sky. Indiscriminate bombs from several US B-52 aircraft blanketed the Earth. She instantly sought shelter beneath the parked vehicle. The brilliantly illuminated landscape quivered as its form was dramatically altered. She was blinded by the incandescent glow, forced to remain hidden until senses of sight and sound torpidly returned to her. Still numb from bewilderment, extreme emotional suspense drove S. P. toward her elder brother. As she gazed toward the western horizon, the expectation of her approaching brother was immensely disappointed. What had been a heroic rescue scene moments before was now replaced by a myriad of disastrous chasms sporadically dotting the landscape. S. P. stumbled into the scalding brush, only to discover her eldest brother and his coworker disemboweled.

Unable to recover the keys from her brother, S. P. was forced to meander toward home in a state of delirium. As she approached her home village, she became resolutely conscious of the scope of the bombing campaign. Fearful that her distressing experience may have also impacted others in her family, she mustered the strength to run the last few kilometers in a desperate effort to reach her home. Despondency quickly replaced any hope within the depths of her heart. Her home had been obliterated along with the vast majority of homes in her village. S. P.'s mother, P., D., and N. were all killed in the bombing raid. Two months later, her brother R. died during another bombing campaign. Consequent to the state of miasma caused by Western bombing initiatives in Cambodia, S. P., her father, and brother S. all joined the forces opposing the bombing raids in the spring of 1967. This faction was known as the Khmer Rouge.

A.2. Royal Government Initiatives

In September 1970, following the military coup installing Lon Nol as the new prime minister of Cambodia, C. volunteered for military service with the Royal Government of Cambodia in Phnom Penh.[2] Subsequent to a dearth of volunteers, C. was quickly promoted to a position with high rank and authority. C. was given the official title of chief financial analyst. Although the weight of this title begs respect and a hint of jealousy, C. insists there was nothing glamorous about his position.

Military funding dollars flowed in from the United States. Official records reflected the growing size of the Royal Army in addition to the dispersion of funds to each soldier. The United States felt an urgency to fund Lon Nol's armies in an effort to combat the encroaching Communists in the northeastern provinces of Cambodia. The same immediacy was not felt by the soldiers themselves. C. remembers a conversation between the force deployment office and the department of finance specifically taking place in order to circumvent the deployment of forces.

The Royal Army went into a defensive mode. Consensus regarding an offensive approach concluded that there would be an unnecessary number of Royal Army casualties.[3] C.'s close friend and neighbor of several years, serving in the strategic operations office, stated: "Let the Khmer Rouge absorb the high deaths, and after the Vietnamese have exhausted their populations, then we will concern ourselves with proactive initiatives."

C.'s job quickly became one of creating phantom soldiers. Financial assistance from the United States was, in part, contingent upon the number of solders fighting for the cause. All that was necessary to receive a bimonthly paycheck from imperialist supporters was the name, birth date, sex, and military identification number of each soldier. Not only were the requirements easy to satisfy, but none of the required information was verified beyond the initial submission. The official size of the Royal Army quickly became a fraction of that reported. C. remembers the proportion of phantom soldiers rising until they comprised 70 to 75% of the payroll. The majority of the $83,000,000 flowing from the United States was subsequently used to line the pockets of the government officials. C. is not proud of the part he played in this travesty. Nonetheless, it did occur.

The full implications of using military funding to create phantom soldiers were not evident until 1973. As the Khmer Rouge grew in number, it began stretching its reach to distant provinces. Despondent villagers migrated toward Phnom Penh as their communities were overtaken by Communist guerillas. Complicating the vast population increases Phnom Penh was experiencing, Khmer Rouge guerillas began instigating combative initiatives on the outskirts of main provincial capitals. The Royal Army, subject to the reality of low soldier counts, dramatically shifted its focus toward conscription efforts. In spite of C.'s job description, the majority of his time was now spent recruiting fighters. Financial compensation was promised to soldiers in exchange for their military service. Due to the unwillingness of military leaders to part with their exorbitant salaries, many newly recruited soldiers began leaving the military and spreading the word regarding its inability to provide pay. C. was, therefore, redirected to oversee the distribution of funding to ensure that all soldiers received their paychecks. C. immediately experienced political pressure from every direction.

Unable to fill the necessary ranks of soldiers, the Royal Army once again employed defensive strategies, specifically the implementation of landmines. Numerous landmines were received, primarily from the United States, following US backing of Prime Minister Lon Nol in a staged coup. Up to this point, the vast majority of landmines had not been used but instead sat dormant in storage. C. wrote correspondence to the United States informing it of the inability of current forces to stop the progressing Khmer Rouge. When additional funding was received, C. paid several nonmilitary personnel to distribute landmines to provincial capitals. Instruction was given to lay the landmines in a fashion that would "best prevent the enemy from overtaking the provincial head." Methods of laying landmines varied drastically between provinces depending on geographic constraints, training of leaders, and the supply of landmines.

The United States began questioning how funds were being used. In a memorandum received in C.'s office, continued military funding from the United States required a more detailed description of the use of funds in addition to a log providing accountability for the past several years. An inevitable scandal came to light, and the Royal Army preempted the possibility of receiving reduced funds from the United States with a declaration of "a corrupt financial analyst" within its ranks. C.'s initial declaration of volunteering for military service quickly came to a close with a "voluntary" admission of abusing his power. He was officially discharged from the service with several permanent black smudges on his record. Unofficially, he was bought off with more than $800,000 and a new identity, a package deal that easily secured retreat into Thailand for him and his family until the Khmer Rouge was no longer in control of the country.

A.3. Khmer Rouge

P. C. was born in Cambodia in 1954.[4] At the age of 8, P. C. accompanied two of his older sisters to a nearby river to fulfill clothes-washing duties for the family. P. C. quickly became bored with domestic chores and climbed into a nearby boat docked on the sandbank. Although P. C. does not remember anything abnormal occurring while he was aboard the small vessel, both sisters adamantly attest that evil spirits visibly made efforts to sink the boat. P. C. was rushed back home to his mother, who was frantic about the episode. Following traditional Cambodian practices, a white string was tied to P. C.'s left wrist to ward off evil spirits. Additionally, P. C.'s mother took the entire contents of a small bowl of rice, placed them in P. C.'s hands, waved his hands around his head three times, and then scattered the rice around his body. It is believed that this custom will bring a wandering spirit back into a body with increased protection and luck. Several events throughout P. C.'s life would require this protection and luck.

In 1973, P. C. turned 19 years old. P. C. remembers the Khmer Rouge gaining strength with each passing month as its presence became more pervasive throughout Cambodia. P. C. was initially conflicted concerning the motives of the Khmer Rouge and a subsequent decision to join its ranks. P. C. had experienced firsthand the corruption of the Lon Nol armies and was vehemently opposed to the capitalist bombing raids. While his knowledge of capitalism was severely flavored with red undertones of mass murder, he was also aware of intolerable acts being committed by the Khmer Rouge. Ultimately, he made a decision to join ranks with the Khmer Rouge in September of 1973.

With intentions to join the tens of thousands of Cambodians declaring allegiance to the Khmer Rouge, P. C. made journey to the nearby provincial capital to attend an orientation meeting.[5] Immediately upon leaving his home, P. C. fell extremely ill and subsequently returned home. Bouts of fever, chills, diarrhea, vomiting, and extreme fatigue restricted P. C. to his home for nearly 6 months following the initial onset of symptoms. Several months into P. C.'s struggle with malaria, decisions to volunteer for service to Ankga[6] were replaced with forced conscription.

O. N., P. C.'s cousin and lifelong friend, devoted much of his time to caring for P. C. until being conscripted February 3, 1974. After O. N. left, P. C. had a firsthand experience that served as a strong motivator to quickly distance himself from the Khmer Rouge. On the morning of February 18, 1974, two armed gunmen showed up at his door, impolitely requesting that their breakfast be prepared by P. C.'s 13-year-old sister P. Over boiled pork and noodles, a verbal investigation ensued concerning P. C.'s reluctance to join Angka's initiative. P. C. insisted he could give nothing to Angka while in his state of physical weakness. The soldiers informed P. C. that he was required to give to Angka in any capacity he could in spite of his poor health. Once again, P. C. contended he had nothing to give. Disputing P. C.'s claim, one soldier tied P. C. to a chair while the other tore the clothes from his sister's body. P. cried out for P. C. not to watch this abhorrent act, a request that was promptly followed. The soldier raping P. poured scalding water left over from boiling the pork for breakfast directly onto P.'s back, instructing P. C. to pay attention to the act being performed. After several minutes of violent rape, the soldiers traded positions, prolonging the torture. As the soldiers left, they told P. C. that every Cambodian has something to give to Angka. "Some choose to give to Angka freely, while others are reluctant. Those reluctant will be reeducated as many times as necessary to willfully give to Angka." P. died several days later from internal bleeding.

Finding an unfamiliar strength, P. C. left his cousin's home on the February 29, just 2 days after the death of his younger sister. Upon arriving in his birth village, P. C. received a warm welcome from his family. Mandatory political meetings were held each night in the new village. Initially, the meetings preached Communist ideals and asked for suggestions from those in attendance. Eventually, however, efforts of purification commenced and practices of declaring faults became the primary activity taking place at meetings. Toward the end of 1975, when the Khmer Rouge had already taken control of the entire country, fault-recognition at village meetings was quickly followed with the disappearance of the accused.[7] Concerns about missing individuals were pacified by responses of reformation and reeducation training programs in distant villages. In early 1976, P. C. was identified at the village meeting for eating vegetables outside the designated meal period. P. C.'s father immediately rebutted the accusation, explaining that P. C. was bringing the vegetables to him. P. C.'s father also added that he consumed the vegetables because he was still hungry after the communal meal.[8] P. C. gathered several belongings to make his escape more comfortable and hid them behind a tree near his hut. P. C. left his village that very night only 1 hour after dusk.

Guards stood watch at the last road leaving town. P. C. decided to hide just out of sight until the eventual changing of guards would allow him to continue his travel. After waiting for nearly an hour, P. C. saw several individuals walking from his village toward the armed guards blocking the road. As faces soon became visible beneath the moonlight, P. C. saw his father standing captive alongside two others from his village. P. C. followed them from a distance as he concocted a plan to assist his father. Several kilometers from the village, the three prisoners were made to kneel alongside a newly trenched ravine with arms bound behind their backs. P. C. snuck closer, finally meeting eyes with his father through the brush. He pulled a paring knife from his bag, suggesting to his father his willingness to free him. With a tear in his eye, P. C.'s father signaled an unwelcome "no" to his son. In a final act of defiance, P. C.'s father began repeating loudly a Cambodian proverb commonplace throughout P. C.'s childhood: "Do good actions, receive good actions; do bad actions, receive bad actions." Perhaps speeding up the inevitable, the guards swung the butt of their rifles against the heads of the three captive Cambodians. As they fell to the ground, a second guard pulled a knife from his boot and slit their throats. Several of the guards simultaneously used their feet to push the lifeless bodies into the ravine.

P. C. lived in the forest for several months after his father died until once again falling ill with malaria. P. C. became so frail that he decided to seek help at a district-level hospital near Phnom Penh. As he traveled toward the hospital, he found a group of slain Khmer Rouge soldiers heaped together in a mountain-like slump. Realizing his chances of receiving treatment for malaria were much better as a Khmer Rouge soldier, P. C. traded clothes with one of the corpses before entering the hospital. P. C. received care for his condition for the next several weeks. When he left the care center, P. C. was given a new military uniform and then escorted by another Khmer Rouge soldier on his way back to a village he inaccurately identified as his post. Making a scheduled stop in the capital, P. C. found himself performing duties with his new coworker to avoid any suspicion of impersonation. They soon arrived at two office-like buildings standing parallel to each other, both active with electricity. Each officer manned a building, waiting for an inbound call that would give information about armament and cars to be received from supporting Communist affiliates outside the country. P. C. waited patiently at his assigned desk for the inbound-only phone to ring. P. C. drifted off to sleep hunched uncomfortably across the desk. When he awoke, dusk had already fallen. He reached for a lantern and attempted to light it. Upon realizing the lantern was empty, he felt around in the dark for some kerosene. Filling the lantern with what he thought must be kerosene, he tilted the lantern slightly to touch the flame of his lighter. Instantly an explosion took place. His lantern exploded into flames immediately, reaching the container that housed gasoline, not kerosene. P. C. attempted to rip his burning clothes off, but his new uniform was strong and very difficult to tear. Eventually, P. C. tore the clothes from his body. He remembers being burnt from head to toe and feeling an extreme cooling sensation often felt with serious burns. P. C.'s military comrade assisted him into the vehicle for immediate transport to the Makara 6 hospital in Phnom Penh. During the drive, P. C. was instructed to blame the explosion on unruly citizens in the village in order to save both of their lives.

After a 2-week stay at the Makara 6 hospital, a sizeable battle broke out between the Khmer Rouge forces and Heng Somrin's[9] soldiers. With a large amount of Vietnamese and Soviet Union armament, Heng Somrin's armies were able to gain control of the capital. Because the vast majority of hospital patients had direct ties with the Khmer Rouge, patients began fleeing the hospital. P. C. was still in critical condition when he left the hospital on May 6, 1978. As Heng Somrin's armies entered the hospital, bodies were lobbed from the fourth floor of the building. Some of the patients, anticipating the massacre of those in the hospital, preempted the attack by pulling pins from grenades and committing suicide. P. C., along with many other hospital patients, attempted to make his way to the nearby train station. Burn scabs on his left heel quickly rubbed off, causing P. C. to crawl the remainder of the way. Each time P. C. felt he could continue no further, a screaming voice from the hospital in the distance reinvigorated his efforts to continue.

The train station was crowded with people waiting to board. When the train arrived, it was too small to accommodate all of the passengers. The train engineers gave preference to individuals with any Chinese heritage, and P. C. was forced to wait for the next train. While P. C. waited near the roadway, his long-lost cousin O. N. drove toward him. P. C. was temporarily relieved that his cousin, now serving as a leader in the Khmer Rouge, would give him a much-needed ride away from the dangerous area. But O. N. informed P. C. that he could not ride with him and drove away. P. C. continued to crawl in the direction of O. N.'s car while crying out for help. While still a considerable distance from the train station, P. C. heard a loud explosion that motivated him to hide in the bushes for several hours. Eventually, P. C. returned to the train station, only to witness the aftermath of another bloody massacre. None of the individuals waiting for the second train were fortunate enough to have lived—except P. C.

Over the next several months, P. C. struggled in solitude to find enough food to survive. He began a long journey toward Thailand, orienting on the setting sun. When he was able to find food and water, he felt his body healing. For a short time, P. C. survived on nothing but small rodents and his own urine. As he approached Battambang, a province near the Cambodia–Thailand border, he was able to join with others who had similar objectives. In November of 1978, P. C. began to travel with a group of nine individuals, of which six were adults and three were children. Late one night, the travelers found themselves nearly crossing paths with an outfit of Khmer Rouge soldiers. In an effort to evade confrontation, they hid beneath banana tree leaves off to the side of the road. As the soldiers approached, a 3-month-old baby girl traveling with them began to cry. The mother attempted to appease the child, but to no avail. Her twin brother also began to cry. A curious soldier began to investigate the situation. The father of the twins quickly suffocated them. The soldier hesitated momentarily and turned away from their hiding spot. After the soldiers left, P. C. mourned the loss of the two babies with the rest of the group.

When P. C. eventually did cross the border into Thailand, he received food and medical attention before being forced back across the border. Tens of thousands of refugees had flooded the relief camps in Thailand. Relief organizations were so overwhelmed with the number of Cambodian refugees that they finally limited the numbers they would accept into their camps. P. C. was a few days too late. Masses of people were forced onto buses and taken to a designated spot and unloaded. Thai soldiers stood guard, anticipating the worst. A few Cambodians began walking across rice fields as instructed by the Thai military personnel. A landmine went off, then a second; soon people were running back toward the border. Guns were pointed at those not obeying orders, and several examples were made. In the fear and confusion, P. C. slipped down a steep ravine backward landing directly on a bamboo shoot. The bamboo shoot entered P. C.'s anus and pierced his spinal cord. P. C. mustered enough strength to crawl toward a soldier, who took pity on him. P. C. was taken back to the camp. No one else was as fortunate.

P. C. came to the United States as a paraplegic in 1989, where he lived for the remainder of his life until dying from health complications at the age of 49. P. C. escaped the Khmer Rouge with his life and nothing more. He built a new life in the United States and found many reasons to continue living. His memory and life lessons live on through his wife and four children, who survive him.

A.4. Thailand Border Protectionists

In 1956, U. P. was born into a lineage of soldiers. Growing up in Thailand's Pathum Thani province, U. P. joined a local militia group at the age of 14.[10] A few months after traveling with the Royal Thai Army, U. P. was assigned the task of repairing engines alongside others who were more experienced at the task. Coming to the aid of a coworker mangled beneath a burning engine, U. P. lost the use of his right hand. He was subsequently removed from active duty and given a courier position with the National News Bureau.[11] U. P.'s duties primarily involved the delivery of newspapers to army headquarters. On occasion, however, U. P. was delivered notification letters of fallen soldiers to surviving family members. The occasional self-pity U. P. felt in regard to his physical handicap was always trumped by what he felt for the family members of slain soldiers.

In 1973, U. P. started delivering military information to several news agencies. Before information was passed on from military posts to the media post, U. P. approved the information through his superior commanding officer. From the beginning of his information exchange, U. P. was aware of the sensitive nature of his position. Relaying false information would quickly compromise his position. Even more important than the veracity of information relayed, however, was the political message passed on to the media from the militaristic standpoint. U. P. began studying the politics of war in Thailand in an effort to understand distinctions between military situations and the media version of national defense initiatives.

The major military matter for Thailand in the 1970s was securing its border against encroaching Communism. U. P. remembers one headline in 1973 reading, "Is Independent Thailand at Risk?" The article went on to boast of the military might Thailand possessed, followed by an outline of securing the Thai–Cambodia border. U. P. remembers being instructed to inflate the number of active military personnel working on securing the border from 24,000 to 150,000. Reports openly admitted landmines were used to secure the border. Distinctions existed, however, between where landmines were being laid by the military and what was being reported to the press. More specifically, the press was informed that villages were cleared prior to laying landmine fields and compensation was given to those uprooted from their homes. In reality, landmines were placed along both sides of the Thai–Cambodia border without regard to civilian residence and with very little compensation for those who were fortunate enough to have been warned. U. P. remembers sitting with circles of military personnel, discussing appropriate measures of hushing the families of those experiencing landmine incidents in order to prevent a potential media surge.[12] U. P. also remembers a decision made by military personnel to shift the focus of landmine placement across to the Cambodian side of the border.

As the Khmer Rouge began a massive agrarian effort in Cambodia, the Royal Thai Army focused even more attention on securing the border. The National News Bureau commissioned U. P. to report on what became known as Thailand's Protective Barrier. After approving the details through the military, U. P. submitted the revised details to the reporting agency. The following day, an article entitled "Thailand's Sovereignty is Secure" in the National News Bureau paper informed the citizens of Thailand about the border situation. The article reads:

> Thailand has once again solidified itself as a sovereign power in Asia. Our Eastern neighbor continues to struggle with Communistic forms of government. The chthonic nature of any of these suppressive regimes however, will not breach beyond our borders. We have humanely ensured our security from our eastern Communist neighbors. More than 150,000 soldiers have worked tirelessly for several years to achieve this great accomplishment. Our powerful military will continue to stand guard across the length of the Thai–Cambodia border by posting soldiers at various checkpoints to warn of any compromising actions by the Communists. Our border cannot be breached. Millions of landmines stand ready to protect our honored country. After our eastern neighbors no longer pose a threat to our country we will remove the landmines from their current positions. Do not be alarmed by these military devices. Your powerful military knows of the whereabouts of each and every explosive device. We have already protected many by paying them to relocate far from the border. Thailand is safe. Thailand is sovereign. Nation, religion and King will exist here forever. (August 16, 1974)

U. P. continued to represent the military by bringing frontline reports to the National News Bureau. He covered numerous political and military stories, unwavering in his approbation for the Royal Thai Army. Uncomfortable with the vast difference between the truth and the printed version of the truth, however, U. P. recorded his original report findings in a notebook he kept hidden.

In November 1977, U. P. attended a celebration party in honor of Thanin Kraivixien, the new prime minister of Thailand. U. P. was introduced to the Prime Minister, as had been arranged by his superior officer. Specifically, U. P. handed Prime Minister Kraivixien a newly composed article endorsing him as the best choice for the leadership of the country. After Prime Minister Kraivixien read the report, U. P. was politely thanked for his hard work on it. The Prime Minister also asked U. P. for the name of his superior officer. U. P. gladly acknowledged Colonel M. R. as his commanding officer, anticipating continued praise. The next day, U. P. was called in by Colonel M. R. U. P. was informed that the Prime Minister felt his handicap was an embarrassment to parliament and was requiring a dismissal from his current position. U. P. was offered low-level military positions, but he rejected them. U. P. defected from the military, severely scathed. A few days later, U. P. appeared at the National News Bureau in full military uniform, pretending to be a figure of authority. He then gave instructions to run an article immediately. U. P. effectively exposed the censorship taking place by first reminding readers of the article printed on August 16, 1974. Next, in a radical step, he introduced himself as the reporting agent and retracted the original article with the following one entitled "The Price of Thailand's Sovereignty." The article reads:

> Thailand has once again solidified itself as a sovereign power in Asia, but at what cost? Cambodia has recently become a Communist country. The spillover from Vietnam into Cambodia makes some question the momentum with which Communism will continue to spread westward. Thailand has adamantly objected to this form of government, stating that Communism is a repressive type of government not suitable in our country. Nearly 25,000 soldiers have been engaged in a two-year long campaign to secure the Thailand–Cambodia border. An invisible barrier, including tens of thousands of landmines and dozens of border guards, guarantees our security from any encroaching Communist offenders.

Although this barrier stands invisible to the enemy, it often stands invisible to our own soldiers as well. Landmines exist beneath the Earth in proximity near the border. Sometimes landmines are on the Thailand side, sometimes across to the Cambodian side. Most of the time, no one knows exactly where the landmines are. In fact, many civilians in Thailand have woken to the surprise of landmines beneath their living quarters. The Royal Thai Army boasts compensation for those living in border regions, simultaneously hushing the multitude of mishaps occurring. Protection from an uncertain enemy has come at the cost of many Thai lives. Perhaps this comes as an innate cost of being Thai.

A.5. Vietnamese-controlled People's Republic of Kampuchea

S. remembers her Khmer Rouge supervisors being approached by other commanding officers at the evening meal on December 26, 1980. She was too far away to hear what was said, but the following day, her entire work group awoke without any Khmer Rouge supervision in its village. She fled immediately. S. had lost her brother to malaria and her mother to malnutrition in the past year, not to mention her initial separation from her three children in the evacuation of Phnom Penh. S. knew in what general direction Phnom Penh lay in relation to her camp thanks to conversations with others in the past several months. Without any physical preparation, S. began the treacherous journey to the capital city in hopes of a reunion with her children. Several days into her meandering trek, she hitched a ride with a passing dump truck headed in her general direction. When S. reached her old home in Phnom Penh, rooms were gutted and walls were only partially standing. Previous photographs, jewelry, letters, and all other valuables were nowhere to be found. She did find enough food in a neighbor's home, however, to enable her to continue for the next several days. After several weeks of regaining strength and hoping for her children to return, she decided to travel to a village several kilometers to the south. S. thought her children might remember how to get to her sister's house more easily than their own because of the simplicity of the road networks. As she journeyed with a few food provisions in hand, she met several others making their way to the Vietnamese border in search of their lost children. S. was informed that when the Vietnamese entered Cambodia, they gathered all orphans into big trucks and shipped them to a holding center near the Cambodia–Vietnam border. This excited S., and she abandoned her previous plans and traveled with her new friends.

They arrived at the Kie Chong orphanage holding center in early March 1980. Hundreds of Cambodian orphans were slowly being nursed back to health within the center. Adults were not allowed to enter the Kie Chong center. Instead, they were provided with the names of their lost children on a form prepared by the Vietnamese officials. S. filled in the form: Sokun, 13, Broh, 9, Serei, 5. After several hours of waiting, S. questioned one of the Vietnamese officials concerning the whereabouts of her children. S. was informed that the process may take time and that she should only concern herself with providing proof of her relationship with the children so when they were found, she would be given guardianship over them. Frustrated that she not only needed proof of her relationship with her children but also that this proof did not exist, she attempted to sneak into the orphanage compound. Immediately upon breaching the outer containment wall, S. was discovered by a Vietnamese official. S. was detained for 16 months before being shipped to an unfamiliar northwestern province of Cambodia named Otdar Mean Chey. S. was involuntary conscripted into national defense projects that eventually included preparing food for K5 workers.

Situations for workers forced to labor on the K5 project were appalling. Food was provisioned once daily, typically allotting a half-cup provision for the entire day. Workers with malaria were often not afforded any special treatment. S. often snuck additional food to young conscripted Cambodians she pitied. In an effort to prevent cooks and food delivery personnel from hoarding food, the Vietnamese required them to wear pocketless uniforms. S. circumvented the safeguard by swallowing additional rice pudding and regurgitating it at a later time, similar to the method a bird uses to feed her young. Cambodians died daily from malaria, diarrhea, starvation, and landmines. Some would be shot in their attempt to escape their work groups. Those who died were shipped to other locations without traditional funeral processions.

On April 27, 1985, S. accompanied a truckload of others to assist in obtaining food provisions just west of the Thailand border. While across the border, S. made her move. Quietly announcing her need to relieve herself, S. snuck down a hillside and kept going. She made her way into a refugee camp, where she stayed until returning with a group of Cambodians forced to repatriate in 1994. S. is still in search of her three missing children.

ENDNOTES

1. Life story interview of S. P. obtained in February 2003.
2. C. has chosen to live by an alias in order to avoid facing consequences of his past actions. Life story interview featuring the person called C. was obtained by author in April 2003.
3. The army was also overcome with an abundance of refugees fleeing from the countryside. This was often used as an excuse not to send soldiers to the conflict zones, in spite of the fact that soldiers did nothing to assist those coming to the city.
4. Information obtained by author in personal interviews with P. C. between the years 1999 and 2000.
5. One of the most influential factors in P. C. deciding to join the Khmer Rouge was the fact that nearly every soldier carried a gun.
6. *Angka* is the Cambodian word for "the organization." The term was used to represent the collective initiative that the Khmer Rouge was supposedly serving. After the fall of the Khmer Rouge, the term became synonymous with Pol Pot.
7. While fault recognition was commonplace and expected of all Cambodians, death took place in secret. Anyone who was an enemy of the revolution was in danger of threatening the cause and was exterminated. Fault recognition was a way of determining who had individualistic ambitions. Those able to think freely were killed.
8. P. C. knows that his father mentioned the consumption of vegetables in conjunction with the inadequacy of the Khmer Rouge to provide for the people of Cambodia because of the severity of this accusation. P. C.'s father knew that the overt act of questioning the Khmer Rouge would make him the target and exonerate P. C. of wrongdoing.
9. Heng Somrin was an army division commander for the Khmer Rouge Communist movement until 1978, when he defected and fled to Vietnam. Heng joined a movement opposing the Khmer Rouge and was backed financially by Vietnam and the Soviet Union.
10. U. P. was stationed with the sixth infantry division of the army, located in the northeast of Thailand beginning in 1970.
11. The National News Bureau in Thailand is the official news agency used by government and its affiliates.
12. Threats and promises backed with power were common methods of convincing families to drop stories about landmine-related incidents.

Appendix B

CMVIS Landmine/UXO Incident Questionnaire Sheet

MINE/ERW CASUALTY REPORT

Serial No. ☐☐☐☐☐ Incident No. ☐☐☐☐☐ - ☐☐ (Fill in one report for each Mine/ERW casualty)

1 General Information

1 **Interviewer** Name__________ Position__________ Province__________

2 **Date of Report:** ☐☐☐☐☐☐ 3 **Date of Incident** ☐☐☐☐☐☐

2 Casualty Information

4 **Full Name:**__________ 5 **Other Name:**__________ 6 **Age:**____ 7 **Sex:** ☐ Male ☐ Female

8 **Family Status:** ☐ Single ☐ Widowed/Divorced ☐ Married 9 If Children, how many? ☐☐

10 **Nationality:** ☐ Cambodian ☐ Thai ☐ Laotian ☐ Vietnamese ☐ Other__________

Contact information

11 Current Address 12 ID Card N° ☐☐☐☐☐☐☐☐☐ 13 Phone N° ☐☐☐☐☐☐☐☐☐☐

#	St	Village	Commune	District	Province

14 How long has the person been living in this village? Month ☐☐ Year ☐☐ 15 V- Code ☐☐☐☐☐☐☐☐

16 Does the person plan to change address? ☐ Yes ☐ No

17 Future Address

#	St	Village	Commune	District	Province

18 V- Code ☐☐☐☐☐☐☐☐

19 **Occupation**

○ Driver ○ Homemaker ○ Daily Laborer ○ Scrap Metal Collector/Refuse Recycler
○ Soldier ○ Police officer ○ Demining worker ○ Child staying at home
○ Farmer ○ Unemployed ○ Civil Servant ○ Student or school child
○ Shopkeeper ○ Woodcutter ○ Construction worker ○ Informal deminer ○ Other__________

3 Activity at the time of incident

20 Was the person on active military duty at the time of the incident? ☐ Yes ☐ No

21 What was the person doing at the time of incident?

- ☐ Handing Mine/ERW →
- ☐ By-stander/ passing by
  - ○ *Watching others handle the ordnance*
  - ○ *Standing or working nearby*
  - ○ Other__________
- ☐ Farming
- ☐ Clearing new land for farming/settlement
- ☐ Collecting food
- ☐ Collecting/cutting wood
- ☐ Herding/tending livestock
- ☐ Making fire
- ☐ Construction
- ☐ Military activity
- ☐ Demining
- ☐ Traveling
- ☐ Going to toilet/defecating/urinating
- ☐ Unknown
- ☐ Other__________

22 ◇ **Motive**

- ○ To make area safe
  - ○ *To clear or expand land*
  - ○ *To prevent accidents for others*
  - ○ *As part of an informal demining activity*
- ○ To fish
- ○ To recover and sell scrap metal
- ○ To re-use as weapon
- ○ To play/curiosity
- ○ Other__________

23 ◇ **Physical interaction with the ordnance**

- ○ Moving it
- ○ Burning it
- ○ Throwing it
- ○ Hitting/striking
- ○ Manual dismantling/refashioning
- ○ None
- ○ Other__________

4 Injury Details

24 From the MINE/ERW incident, was the casualty ☐ Killed ☐ Injured

25 If the casualty died, how long after the incident? ☐ Immediately hours ☐☐ days ☐☐ weeks ☐☐

26 Where did the casualty die?

☐ At site of incident ☐ On the way to health facility ☐ Unknown

☐ In health facility/hospital ☐ At home/after leaving health facility ☐ Other: ____________

27 Amputation?

	Arm	ForeArm	Hand	Thumb	Finger	AKA	BKA	Foot	FirstToe	Toe	Genitals
Right	☐	☐	☐	☐	☐	☐	☐	☐	☐	☐	☐
Left	☐	☐	☐	☐	☐	☐	☐	☐	☐	☐	

		Face	Upper Limb	Upper Body	Lower Limb	Lower Body
28 Wounds?	Right	☐	☐	☐	☐	☐
	Left	☐	☐	☐	☐	☐
29 Burns?	Right	☐	☐	☐	☐	☐
	Left	☐	☐	☐	☐	☐
30 Paralysis?	Right	☐	☐	☐	☐	☐
	Left	☐	☐	☐	☐	☐

31 Deafness?

	Partial	Total
Right	☐	☐
Left	☐	☐

32 Eyes

	Partially blind	Totally blind
Right	☐	☐
Left	☐	☐

5 Emergency medical care

33 Did the casualty reach one or more medical facility ? ☐ Yes ☐ No ☐ Ukn Go to Section 6

Name	Type	Time until medical facility reached					Medical services received	
		<30min	<60min	< 2 hrs	> 2 hrs	days	Yes	No
		☐	☐	☐	☐	☐☐	☐	☐
		☐	☐	☐	☐	☐☐	☐	☐
		☐	☐	☐	☐	☐☐	☐	☐

Response options for "Type"

1 Health Post, 2 Private Clinic 3 Health centre 4 Referral Hospital 5 National Hospital

6 Mine/ERW Awareness

34 Did the casualty receive MRE prior to the incident? ☐ Yes ☐ No ☐ Unknown

GO TO Question 35

		Received	Frequency: Once	Several times	Regularly
39	Poster/leaflet	☐	☐	☐	☐
40	TV	☐	☐	☐	☐
41	Radio	☐	☐	☐	☐
42	School	☐	☐	☐	☐
43	Community meeting	☐	☐	☐	☐
44	Door to door	☐	☐	☐	☐
45	Community liaison	☐	☐	☐	☐
46	Other	☐	☐	☐	☐

Describe: ____________

35 How often did the casualty go to the incident area ?

☐ First time ☐ Several times

☐ Regularly ☐ Unknown

☐ Other: ____________

36 Did the casualty know there was Mine/ERW at the incident site ?

☐ Yes ☐ No ☐ Unknown

37 Why did the casualty enter the incident area?

☐ Economic necessity ☐ Curiosity ☐ No other access ☐ Unknown ☐ Other: ____________

Updated: November, 2007 for 2008 version 5.0

Interview 1

38 Date of interview: ☐☐☐☐☐☐ Day/Month/Year

Location of interview

39 Address

#	St	Village:	Commune:	District:	Province:

40 Place of interview ☐ Health facility, Name:________ ☐ Private house
☐ Police Station, Name:________ ☐ Other Describe:________

Informant 41 Name: ____________ 42 Phone N° ☐☐☐☐☐☐☐☐☐☐

43 Address

#	St	Village:	Commune:	District:	Province:

44 Type of informant ☐ Victim ☐ Relative/Family ☐ Village Chief ☐ Health worker
☐ Demining worker ☐ Police ☐ Military ☐ Community member

45 Section(s): 1☐ 2☐ 3☐ 4☐ 5☐ 6☐ 46 Reliability of Informant: ☐ Low ☐ Average ☐ High

Interview 2

47 Date of interview: ☐☐☐☐☐☐ Day/Month/Year

Location of interview

48 Address

#	St	Village:	Commune:	District:	Province:

49 Place of interview ☐ Health facility, Name:________ ☐ Private house
☐ Police Station, Name:________ ☐ Other Describe:________

Informant 50 Name: ____________ 51 Phone N° ☐☐☐☐☐☐☐☐☐☐

52 Address

#	St	Village:	Commune:	District:	Province:

53 Type of informant ☐ Victim ☐ Relative/Family ☐ Village Chief ☐ Health worker
☐ Demining worker ☐ Police ☐ Military ☐ Community member

54 Section(s): 1☐ 2☐ 3☐ 4☐ 5☐ 6☐ 55 Reliability of Informant: ☐ Low ☐ Average ☐ High

Interview 3

56 Date of interview: ☐☐☐☐☐☐ Day/Month/Year

Location of interview

57 Address

#	St	Village:	Commune:	District:	Province:

58 Place of interview ☐ Health facility, Name:________ ☐ Private house
☐ Police Station, Name:________ ☐ Other Describe:________

Informant 59 Name: ____________ 60 Phone N° ☐☐☐☐☐☐☐☐☐☐

61 Address

#	St	Village:	Commune:	District:	Province:

62 Type of informant ☐ Victim ☐ Relative/Family ☐ Village Chief ☐ Health worker
☐ Demining worker ☐ Police ☐ Military ☐ Community member

63 Section(s): 1☐ 2☐ 3☐ 4☐ 5☐ 6☐ 64 Reliability of Informant: ☐ Low ☐ Average ☐ High

Note:

____

____

____

____

OFFICE USE ONLY	Receipt date	Form checked by	Computer entry by	Entry checked by

Updated: August, 2007 for 2008 version 5.0

Appendix C

Metal Price Record

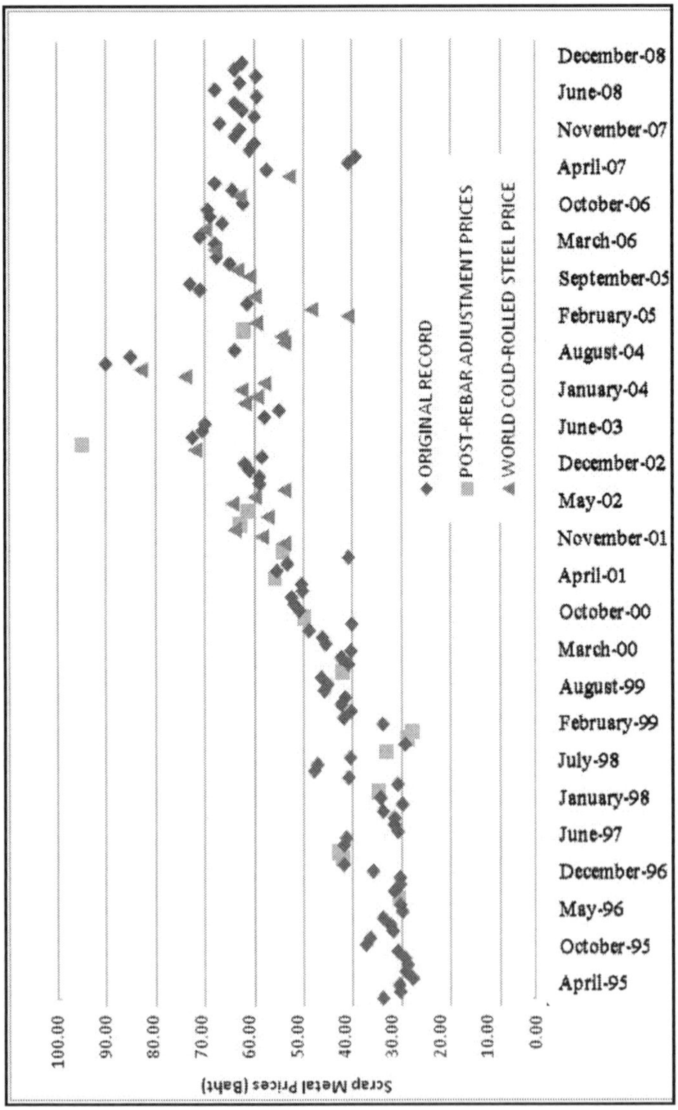

Appendix D
Research Memoir

Rebar being sorted according to size and grade prior to being sold to construction warehouses in Pailin Cambodia.

Author Wade Roberts with a team of formal landmine/UXO deminers employed by the Royal Government of Cambodia. This team was tasked with clearing the first 50 meters on both sides of a well-used roadway in a town near the Cambodia-Vietnam border.

Author's wife, Cindy Roberts, enjoying time with Cambodian children.

Author Wade Roberts interviewing Bo Pith, a landmine survivor, amputee, and mine-risk education advocate living in Svay Rieng, Cambodia.

Author Wade Roberts with Bong Cheng Lo, a project manager working for the Cambodian Mine/UXO Victim Information System (CMVIS) in Phnom Penh, Cambodia.

Author Wade Roberts discussing trends in landmine-related incidents with CMVIS managing director, Chhiv Lim.

Author Wade Roberts confirming metal price consistencies with scrap yards positioned along the Cambodia-Vietnam border. Picture taken with Bo Stoun, the yard master and owner of the pictured scrap yard, who splits his time between selling scrap metal to Vietnam and farming rice.

Author Wade Roberts interviewing a Buddhist monk in Southwestern Cambodia. The pictured dinner bell is a hollowed out explosive parcel (perhaps the most constructive use ever made of an explosive remnant of war).

Visit to a large scrap yard on the Thailand-Cambodia border with the local Cambodian Mine/UXO Action Center (CMAC) administrative head. Metal was sorted and heaped prior to being loaded on trucks, weighed, and shipped across the Thai border.

The pictured remnants of war were discovered by three young male scrappers working in Battambang province, Cambodia. This ordnance was collected and sold weekly to a middle-level transporter that made journey toward the Thai side of the country.

Explosive ordnance pictured here still contains TNT. This picture was taken at one of the final scrap yards that exists very near the Cambodia-Thailand border on the Cambodian side—proof that ordnance is brought near the border before being decased or "tampered" with.

Metal arriving at any of the final scrap yards near the Cambodia-Thailand border is first sorted into ordnance and non-ordnance piles. Following this initial sorting process, ordnance is then sifted through in an effort to divide the "live" ordnance from that which has already been sufficiently tampered with to be considered safe. Live ordnance is either reported to CMAC or contracted out to individuals willing to take on this risk.

Ordnance comes in many shapes and sizes.

This ordnance was heaped into a pile immediately after being cleaned from explosives. Before selling this ordnance across the border, the parcels need to be broken apart in order to become indistinguishable from other metal scraps. Selling ordnance across the border is illegal.

A young boy pries a metal casing open. Each ordnance component can facilitate separate market transactions. A market exists specifically for the metal, fuses, and explosives.

A reminder of the residual impact of war more than 30 years later.

Explosive remnants of war are often heaped into piles based on whether they still contain explosives. The heat in Cambodia often makes the tampering process even more risky.

Young boys discuss their approach to collecting scrap for the day. Agreements are made to split the find equally among each member of the group. The boys expressed excitement over the potential find because it meant they could afford soda and gum.

References

Asia Watch: Physicians for Human Rights [AWPHR]. (1991). Landmines in Cambodia: The Coward's War. New York: Asia Watch / Human Rights Watch.

Bottomley, R. (2001). The K5 gamble: National defense and national building under the People's Republic of Kampuchea. *Journal of Southeast Asian Studies*, *32*(2), 195–210.

Bottomley, R. (2003). Balancing risk: Village demining in Cambodia. *Third World Quarterly*, *24*(5), 823–837.

Brown, M. and J. Zasloff (1998). *Cambodia confounds the peacemakers, 1979–1998*. New York: Cornell University Press.

Cambodian Mine Victim Information System (CMVIS). (2008). *Landmine/UXO incident statistics*. Phnom Penh: Cambodian Mine Action Authority.

Cixous, H. (1994). *The terrible but unfinished story of Norodom Sihanouk, King of Cambodia*. Lincoln: University of Nebraska Press.

Courtois, S. (1999). *The black book of communism: Crimes, terror, repression*. Cambridge: Harvard University Press.

Duncanson, D., Ponchaud, F., & Amphoux, N. (January 01, 1979). Review of Cambodia Year Zero. *International Affairs (royal Institute of International Affairs 1944-), 55,* 1, 167–168.

East-West Management Institute [EWMI] (2001). *Land law in Cambodia*. Phnom Penh, Cambodia: Asian Development Bank.

Gottesman, E. (2003). *Cambodia after the Khmer Rouge: Inside the politics of nation building.* New Haven & London: Yale University Press.

Harris, G. (2000). The economics of landmine clearance: Case study of Cambodia. *Journal of International Development*, *12*, 219–225.

International Campaign to Ban Landmines. (2006). *Landmine monitor report*. Geneva, Switzerland: Landmine Monitor.

Keeley, R. (2006). *The economics of landmine clearance*. London: University of London Press.

L'Histoire terrible mais inachevée de Norodom Sihanouk, roi du Cambodge, 1985; as The Terrible but Unfinished Story of Norodom Sihanouk, King of Cambodia, translated by Juliet Flower MacCannell, Judith Pike, and Lillie Groth, 1994.

Martin, M. A. (1989). *Cambodia: A shattered society*. Berkeley and Los Angeles: University of California Press.

McGrath, R. (1994). *Landmines: Legacy of conflict: A manual for development workers*. Oxford: Oxfam Print Unit.

Metal Prices and News on the Internet (2009, May 28). Historical Price Records. Retrieved from www.metalprices.com.

Ministry of Agriculture (MOA). (2008a). *Agricultural harvest yield tables*. Phnom Penh: Ministry of Agriculture.

Ministry of Agriculture (MOA). (2008b). *Cambodia agriculture statistics*. Phnom Penh: Ministry of Agriculture.

Moyes, R. (2004). *Tampering: Deliberate handling & use of live ordnance in Cambodia.* Phnom Penh: Handicap International–Belgium.

Moyes, R. (2005). *A study of scrap metal collection in Lao PDR*. Geneva: GICHD.

National Institute of Statistics [NIS]. (1999). *1998 General census of Cambodia*. Phnom Penh: Cambodia Press.

National Institute of Statistics [NIS]. (2004a). *Cambodian socioeconomic survey*. Phnom Penh: Cambodian Press.

National Institute of Statistics [NIS]. (2004b). *Population projections for Cambodia 1998–2020*. Phnom Penh: Center for Population Studies.

National Institute of Statistics [NIS]. (2006). *State of the economy report*. Phnom Penh: Southeast Asian Press.

National Institute of Statistics [NIS]. (2007). *China exports volumes and practices*. Bejing: China Government.

Royal Government of Cambodia [RGC] (1999). *1998 General census of Cambodia*. Phnom Penh: Cambodia Press.

Slocomb, M. (2001). K-5 gamble. *Journal of Southeast Asian Studies*, *32*(2), 195.

Tobler, W. (1970). *A computer movie simulating urban growth in the detroit region.* Detroit: Economic Geography.

United Nations. (1999). International Campaign to Ban Landmines, Landmine Monitor Report. Toward a Mine-Free World. New York: Human Rights Watch.

United Nations. (2005). International Campaign to Ban Landmines, Landmine Monitor Report. (2005). Toward Mine-Free World. New York: Human Rights Watch.

U.S. Department of State. (1992). 1998 Hidden Killers: The Global Landmine Crisis. Bureau of Political-Military Affairs, Office of Humanitarian Demining Programs.

Further Reading

Banister, J. and Johnson, E. P. (1993). After the nightmare: The population of Cambodia. In B. Kiernan (Ed.), *Genocide and democracy in Cambodia: The Khmer Rouge, the United Nations, and the international community*. New Haven, Conn: Yale University Southeast Asia Studies.

Boutros-Ghali, B. (January 01, 1994). The Land Mine Crisis: A Humanitarian Disaster. *Foreign Affairs, 73,* 5.)

Chandler, D. P. (1996). *A history of Cambodia*. Boulder Colo: Westview Press.

Eaton, B. (January 01, 2003). Crisis, containment and development: the role of the landmine impact survey. *Third World Quarterly - Journal of Emerging Areas, 24,* 5, 909–921.

Harpviken, K. B., Horwood, C., & McGrath, R. (January 01, 2003). Guides to Humanitarian Mine Action. *Third World Quarterly, 24,* 5, 967–976.

Kiernan, B. (1996). *The Pol Pot regime: Race, power, and genocide in Cambodia under the Khmer Rouge, 1975-79*. New Haven: Yale University Press.

Kiernan, B., & Boua, C. (1982). *Peasants and politics in Kampuchea, 1942-1981*. London: Zed Press.

Jackson, K. D. (January 01, 1978). Cambodia 1977: Gone to Pot. *Asian Survey, 18,* 1, 76–90.

Lal, V. (January 01, 1995). Little Merchants of War: Land Mines as Sentinels of Death. *Economic and Political Weekly, 30,* 14, 739.

McClelland, J. (January 01, 2005). Conventional Weapons: A Cluster of Developments. *International and Comparative Law Quarterly, 54,* 3, 755–767.

Moore, E. (January 01, 1989). Water Management in Early Cambodia: Evidence from Aerial Photography. *Geographical Journal, 155,* 2, 204–214.

Neupert, R., & Prum, V. (January 01, 2005). Cambodia: Reconstructing the Demographic Stab of the Past and Forecasting the Demographic Scar of the Future. *European Journal of Population, 21,* 2–3.

Nixon, R. (November 01, 2007). Of Land Mines and Cluster Bombs. *Cultural Critique, 67,* 1, 160–174.

O'Kane, R. H. T. (January 01, 1993). Cambodia in the Zero Years: Rudimentary Totalitarianism. *Third World Quarterly, 14,* 4, 735–748.

Poole, P. A. (January 01, 1976). Cambodia 1975: The Grunk Regime. *Asian Survey, 16,* 1, 23–30.

Skara, B. A. (January 01, 2003). Risky business or constructive assistance? Community engagement in humanitarian mine action. *Third World Quarterly - Journal of Emerging Areas, 24,* 5, 839–853.

Tuon, B. (January 01, 2004). Cambodia: Memory and Desire. *The Massachusetts Review, 45,* 3, 319.

Vickery, M. (1984). *Cambodia, 1975–1982.* Boston: South End Press.

Walque, D. (January 01, 2005). Selective Mortality during the Khmer Rouge Period in Cambodia. *Population and Development Review, 31,* 2, 351–368.

Walque, D. (January 01, 2006). The socio-demographic legacy of the Khmer Rouge period in Cambodia. *Population Studies, 60,* 2, 223–231.

Index

Made in the USA
Monee, IL
12 November 2026

70dba070-288d-4bf5-9a6b-9fe98367e5fdR01